Contents

Acknowledgements

■

I would like to thank a number of people who helped me in the writing of this book. Firstly, Vanessa Helps, who suggested that I should write it in the first place. Susan Leeming, Jackie Kereszteny, Deirdre Tidy and Tricia Boyle, who read various drafts and made suggestions and comments. Catherine Trew created the illustrations and patiently put up with late amendments and additions. Last but not least, Phil, Joanna and Peter, who gave me support, encouragement and time when I needed it.

Preface

■

I believe that very few people read books about management skills from cover to cover. Consequently, while the book can be read from beginning to end, and is structured in that way, I hope it will also be easy to 'dip in', to find the information you need most, at the time when you need it.

I have used 'he' and 'him', 'she' and 'her' as equally as possible through the book, without being structured enough to have 'hims' in one chapter and 'hers' in another. Please read 'she' for 'he' and 'he' for 'she' where appropriate.

1

Negotiating – an everyday event

You have been negotiating ever since you were old enough to disagree with your parents about whether or not you should eat your cabbage. We all negotiate, every day, with our workmates, partners, children, friends and acquaintances. Most of the time we might not even be aware that we are doing it because it is such an everyday event.

What is negotiating? What is the difference between negotiating and other forms of meeting or communicating? Let's have a definition.

Negotiation involves an element of trade or bargaining – an exchange of one valuable resource for another to enable both parties to achieve a satisfactory outcome.

1

Often, we fail to realise that many of the transactions that we engage in every day are a form of negotiation. Some of them are fixed negotiations where we wouldn't even think of trying to bargain, such as paying for a carton of apple juice in the supermarket. In other similar situations though, we might try to bargain. If the pair of trousers we chose from the department store had a button missing, we might ask for a discount. If we were buying a similar pair of trousers from a tailor in Hong Kong, we might not just ask for a discount, but engage in some haggling before reaching an agreed price.

Other negotiations which we carry out everyday, maybe without thinking about them, may range from agreeing with a colleague as to who should do a particular piece of work, the most convenient date for a group to meet again, or who will collect whose children from school today.

In fact, many people prefer to negotiate. They don't like asking favours and doing or giving nothing in return; neither do they like to feel that they are doing something for nothing. If you ask your neighbours to look after your house while you are on holiday, you may feel under an obligation to them. Perhaps you bring them back a present from your holiday, but may not feel that you have discharged your obligation until they ask the same favour from you. A sense of 'fair play' is often present in our most informal relationships. So what's the problem? If you've been doing it all this time, what are you worried about? Why isn't it easy?

The reason that it isn't always easy, why sometimes it looks or feels as if it's going to be a problem, is that from the cabbage negotiation on through the bedtime, home from the party time, borrowing the car time, getting the report finished on time negotiations, you may not have always felt that the outcome was an acceptable one for you. You didn't always win. Sometimes you may have felt as if you invariably lost.

For some people, the very fact that the transaction they are about to undertake is labelled with the name 'A Negotiation' means that they become nervous and concerned about it. This book aims to make it easier to treat negotiating as a common or garden everyday event. By making it more comfortable and easy to negotiate, it will be easier for you to achieve a result that is pleasing both to you and to the other people involved.

WHAT MAKES A GOOD NEGOTIATOR?

Late one night, while drifting off to sleep, I heard a reporter on the radio say: 'The Chinese are past masters at negotiating, they are resourceful, patient and ruthless.' So do we need to be like the Chinese in order to be successful negotiators?

Resourceful and patient – definitely. Ruthless? I think successful negotiators are not ruthless, because being ruthless means that you disregard the needs of the other party in order to meet your own. Substitute the words persistent, determined or firm and you have a pretty good description of a successful negotiator. So to be a skilful and successful negotiator, you need to be:

RESOURCEFUL

PATIENT

FIRM

RESOURCEFUL   Good negotiators need to be able to deal with lots of constantly changing information and uncertainty. Having things decided and settled straightaway is not the way to get the best deal out of a situation, so it is useful to have the ability to live with and thrive in situations where you don't know quite what is going to happen next. This is where the ability to think and respond rapidly becomes important.

PATIENT   Negotiators need to be patient, mainly because the blunt instrument approach to negotiating tends to have a limited and short term effect. Pushing or bludgeoning the other negotiator towards a solution can have the effect of making them more stubborn or unmoving. Pulling them towards a solution may involve more time, more tolerance and persistence, but is more likely to achieve a satisfactory and lasting outcome.

FIRM   Negotiators need to be firm because it may be necessary to stand your ground against aggressive or blunt-instrument style negotiators. It is important to be sure of your desired outcome and the concessions you are prepared to make in order to achieve it. You also need to know the point at which you are prepared to walk away – the point at which you will stop negotiating because you are not prepared to meet the terms demanded.

THE PROCESS OF NEGOTIATING

If we look at the bare bones of the process of negotiation, a simplistic notion of the negotiating stages is expressed in Fig. 1.1. This is a simplistic representation of a meeting which involves not just the motivations, needs and skills of the people or groups involved, but a wide variety of peripheral issues, including the power balance, the environment and culture in which the negotiation is taking place, and any previous history of contact, conflict or expectation.

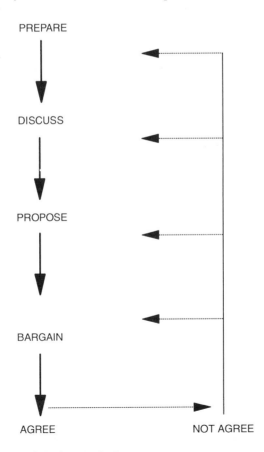

3

Fig. 1.1 The process of negotiating

A more realistic representation of the process can be envisaged from Fig 1.2. When you are negotiating, many things are happening at once – you have to cope with considering and stating your own needs, while at the same time trying to pick up all the direct and subtle signals and

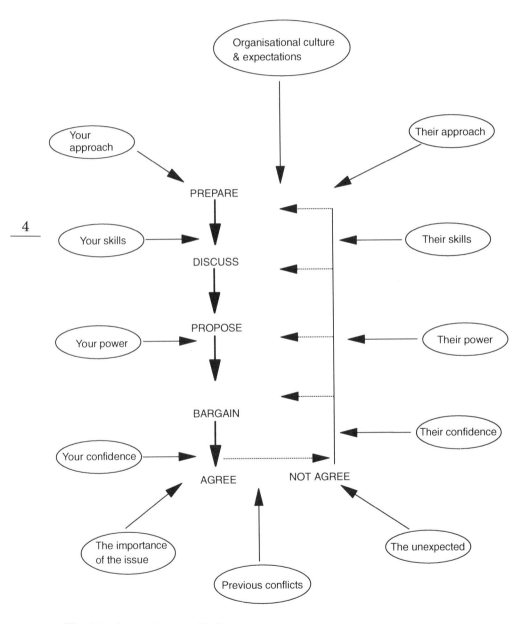

Fig. 1.2 Contraints and influences on the process of negotiating

nuances originating from the persons with whom you are negotiating. You have to ensure that you understand exactly what they are saying, can translate it into what it might mean to you and then react to it quickly and coherently. No wonder people get worried about it.

BUILDING A RAPID RESPONSE MECHANISM

In order to cope with the multitude of sensory and factual information to be processed, digested and responded to in a negotiation, you need a Rapid Response Mechanism, that is, the ability to sort and prioritise information and react to it in appropriate and effective ways. Unfortunately, acquiring a Rapid Response Mechanism is not a simple matter of saying, 'I'll have one of those please', and taking it off the shelf. Nor is it a question of learning one particular skill. If it were, negotiating would be easy and there would be no need for books and courses.

However, it is possible to acquire a rapid response mechanism by bringing together a number of skills and by increasing awareness. A rapid response mechanism is built on various foundations and relies on certain essential skills. These are shown in Table 1.1. You can train yourself to be able to respond more quickly and effectively in negotiations. In order to do so, you need to ensure that your foundations are sound and that your essential skills are polished.

5

Table 1.1 Foundations and skills

Foundations for thinking on your feet	Essential skills for rapid responses
A problem-solving approach Preparation Awareness of power Confidence Basic knowledge of strategies and tactics	Real listening Creative questioning Extended thinking

Figure 1.3 is a representation of the process of bargaining once the skills, approach and confidence of a rapid response mechanism begin to influence it.

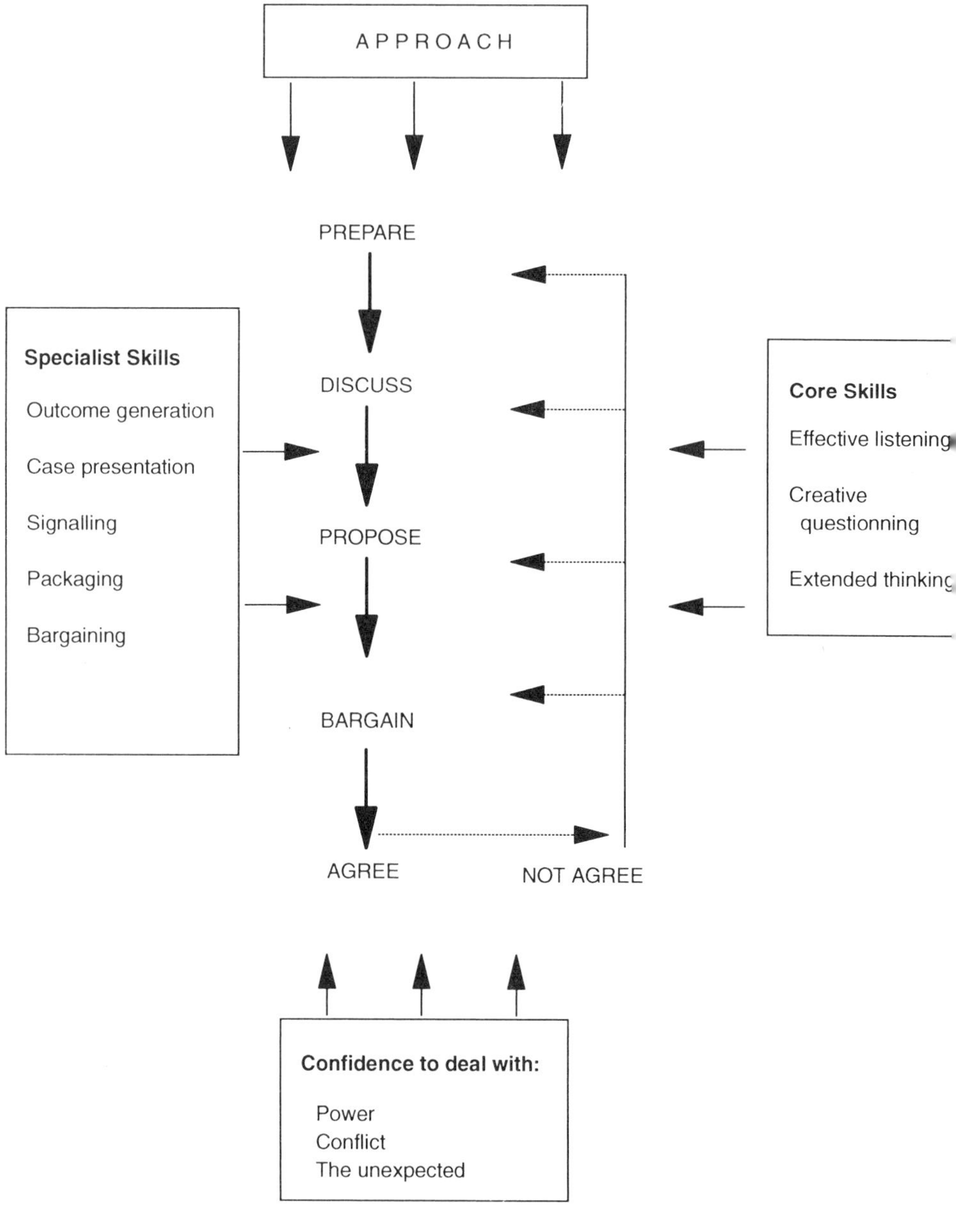

6

Fig. 1.3 Building a rapid response mechanism

BARRIERS TO DEVELOPING A RAPID RESPONSE MECHANISM

Patterns

The negotiations you have been involved with in the past may have followed a pattern. Organisations tend to have accepted norms of negotiating, not just who is authorised to negotiate with whom over what, but the way people go about it. Fledgling negotiators learn from more experienced negotiators – by observation or hearsay. The negotiations we hear about through the media also appear to have a pattern – one which often involves the breakdown of those negotiations at some point.

Therefore, many people, observing the behaviour of other more experienced negotiators, see the patterns, learn from them and use those patterns, which eventually become their own habitual behaviours. In order to learn to be a better, faster-reacting negotiator, you may need to unlearn some of the patterns and habits you have acquired in life so far. Even if you believe that you are a complete novice at negotiation, don't fool yourself. Remember the day-to-day stuff? You will have absorbed some patterns.

7

Cultural norms in negotiating

Some cultures have different expectations for negotiators to others. The most obvious example of this is the difference between buying goods in a country where bargaining is part of the fun of shopping, and a country where the marked price is the one you are expected to pay.

This is also the case in different organisations. In one organisation, managers may be expected to negotiate with no quarter given or expected. In another, a 'gentlemanly' approach may be expected, where managers are expected to be prepared to get less than they would like. Operating in a way which does not fit cultural norms may lead to distressed and disgruntled players.

LEARNING TO THINKING ON YOUR FEET

Ask yourself 'Why am I negotiating?' (and why are they negotiating with me?)

Why are you negotiating rather than just going ahead and doing what you want? It's a good question to ask yourself because it can help you to focus on tactics and strategies. There may well be a number of very good reasons why you are negotiating, but they may vary from negotiation to negotiation. Some of them may be:

- you don't have the power to go ahead and just do it
- you don't want to appear to be a dictator
- other people have to cooperate in order to achieve your outcome and they have equal power and equally strong opinions
- you prefer to have some democracy in your management style
- you want to set a good example
- you're building up credit for the future
- you know that you will have to give something away in order to achieve what you want.

Whatever your reason for negotiating, it is useful to be aware of it – it is the basis for the whole process. Knowing your reason for negotiating is one of the foundations for your desired outcome – an essential part of your preparation. It is also a big help if at any stage you need to make the decision to stop negotiating. There are situations where negotiating might not be the most appropriate way to settle an issue and it is important to recognise this, so that you will be comfortable with making the decision to refuse to negotiate or to walk away from a negotiation.

Extend your brain

Thinking on your feet in negotiations means being able to process all the data in a coherent way, and then react appropriately. How can a book help you to do that? Surely you need a brain extension?

This book can help you to provide your own brain extension and develop a rapid response mechanism by exploring some different ways to enhance your thinking and stretch it in different and interesting directions in order to increase your ability to react quickly and effectively in negotiations. It does not necessarily provide any entirely new ideas about how to negotiate, just different and extra ways to help you think differently and more creatively about the process. 'The real voyage of discovery consists not in seeking new lands but in seeing with new eyes', (Proust).

This book aims to examine a number of the issues around negotiating, using the best of the acknowledged, tried and tested methods. However, it will look at some of them in a new light to see how you might break or extend your habitual patterns to encompass additional ways of thinking and reacting. This does not mean changing your thinking but extending it. Some of the specific areas covered are:

1 Taking a new look at preparation to make sure you really are prepared, not just think you are. This means looking at your approach to the negotiation and your desired outcome; thinking about what you want and how to achieve it.

2 Looking at how to achieve rapport in ways which might not have occurred to you, but are simple to use.

3 Identifying ways to increase your confidence as a negotiator and examining how your confidence permeates through to the way you present your case and react to others, and how it can affect the outcome of the negotiation.

4 Thinking about the balance of power involved in negotiating and how you can make the most of the power you have.

5 Identifying the strategies and tactics which are most useful or feel most right for you to use.

6 Identifying essential bargaining skills and how to use them most effectively.

7 Thinking about extending your questioning, listening and thinking skills so that they become real tools for quick reactions.

8 Thinking about how you might react to stalemates, or the unexpected. Showing you ways to react calmly and productively in these situations rather than feeling thrown or threatened.

9 Looking at conflict and how it relates to both the need for and the process of negotiating.

10 Focusing on ways of ensuring that you learn positive and valuable lessons from your negotiating experiences, so that you can put them into practice and continuously improve.

LEARNING TO BECOME A BETTER NEGOTIATOR

When you start moving along the road to becoming a better negotiator, certain core skills such as listening, questioning and thinking need to be learned, or polished and brought into active use. Other specialist skills such as preparation, case presentation, bargaining and packaging can be learned. Some of these skills are essential to doing even a mediocre job: to do a good job you need to be able to use them all. The peripheral elements such as power, conflict, etc need to be considered, so that you operate in a way that fits the environment. But the first thing to consider in any negotiation, the issue which sets the scene and creates the flavour for the whole event is your approach. Let us start by looking at Approach.

2

A positive approach

Elizabeth and her father run a building business. When talking to Elizabeth about writing this book, she told me about her father's approach to negotiating.

'He always tries to get the most he possibly can out of the other party. He takes a very aggressive approach and tries to give away as little as possible while pinning down the other person to a deal which gives him what he wants, but sometimes means that they end up with a pretty raw deal. It's counter productive really, because you usually end up dealing with the same person more than once. The second time you meet them, they are much less cooperative and more wary about doing business with you. I tell him that he ought to try taking a less aggressive approach, but he won't listen – he thinks you have to be tough to negotiate successfully.'

If you ask a group to call out the words they associate with the word Negotiation, many of the answers they call out will have an aspect of competition, some will have the flavour of a fight or war. The concept of battle being joined is pervasive. Many of the negotiations which come to public notice do seem to have an aggressive element to them, with the two sides entrenched in their seemingly unalterable positions.

There is another way. Instead of looking at a negotiation as two opposing parties, needing to fight their way towards a compromise, look at it as two people or groups, each with a problem which needs to be solved. Fisher and Ury, in *Getting to Yes*, (1981), identify positional bargaining as one of the things which cause negotiations to break down. When people lock themselves into a position, they often pay less attention to meeting their real needs than to achieving a solution as near as possible to their starting position.

The difference between Problem Solving and the Problem-Solving Approach

Using a problem-solving approach to negotiating does not mean treating each negotiation as a problem-solving exercise. What is the difference?

PROBLEM SOLVING

If you are simply problem solving, you are likely to set out all the problems and difficulties, possibilities and ideas at the beginning of the exercise, and expect your colleague to do the same. If you do this inappropriately, when the other or others concerned may have different objectives from you, then you may find at the end of the session that their objectives are met and yours are not. Take three departments which between them need to cut 10 per cent of their staff. Two of the department heads come to the meeting prepared to negotiate. The third comes prepared to problem solve. He suggests that they each cut their staff complement by 10 per cent and volunteers the information about the staff he intends to cut. The other two are likely to spend some time helping him to make further cuts in his staff complement as he can obviously afford to do so, while making the strongest possible case for keeping the maximum number of their own staff.

THE PROBLEM-SOLVING APPROACH

When you use a problem-solving approach to negotiating, you are prepared to negotiate, but your approach is one which will help to achieve a solution as satisfactory as possible to both parties, rather than one which helps to maintain as much of your original position as possible. The key points about the problem-solving approach are:

- a collaborative rather than a competitive climate is created
- you look on it as a problem to be solved rather than a battle to be won
- you aim to get both parties working together to solve the problem
- a WIN–WIN outcome is achieved

The skills and strategies we will be exploring in this book can be used most effectively with a problem-solving approach. While it is possible to use many of them in aggressive and manipulative ways, you are likely to achieve more of what you want and attain more lasting results if you do use a problem-solving approach.

TAKING A TOUGH LINE

Can you take a problem-solving approach without seeming to be a bit of a softy, or worse, a pushover? If you are concerned with helping your opponent to solve his/her problems, won't that mean that he/she is going to be able to manipulate you into giving them what they want. Doesn't it mean that you open yourself up to other people walking all over you? Not necessarily.

Taking a problem-solving approach doesn't mean that you have to be soft with it. It means that you need to know what your desired outcome is and what your motivation behind that outcome might be, but you can be as tough as you like in trying to achieve a solution to the problem. A solution to the problem will mean that you have achieved if not all, then quite a lot of what you want. What's soft about that?

Why is the Problem-Solving Approach important?

When thinking about the approach you will use to the negotiation you are about to undertake, and the strategies you might use to get what you want, remember a few important facts:

You will probably have to live with that person, or work with that group, or deal with that client again in the future

People have long memories, especially for times when they feel they have not been treated fairly in some way. Many people, if they feel that they have been cheated, or humiliated or swindled, will consciously or unconsciously have the attitude 'I'll get you for that one day' or 'You owe me one for that and I'm going to make sure you don't get the better of me next time'.

So if John scores a triumphant success in one negotiation, but Sally feels that it was not done fairly, or that she was bullied or humiliated, or that she let John get away with too large a slice of the cake, next time they deal together she is likely to want to 'get her own back'. Whether she does so or not will depend on her skill and possibly on how unscrupulous she is prepared to be – maybe she will go away feeling satisfied that scores have been settled – or possibly feeling even more aggrieved, with a bigger chip on her shoulder.

The other person involved has wants, needs and a desired outcome for this negotiation

When two people come to a negotiation, they usually both feel that they have a good case and that they want to get the best deal they can from the meeting. Each person may think that right is on their side, that they have a good case for their proposals or demands.

Therefore, if Sally concentrates only on the outcome she wants from the negotiation, ignoring or forgetting the outcome John may want, she is running the risk of bringing a lot more conflict into the situation than may be necessary. If John feels that she is ignoring his needs, he may become more aggressive in pursuing them. Alternatively, he may refuse to negotiate.

Your behaviour now will set up expectations for your behaviour in the future

Whatever John's reaction at the time, he will remember that Sally was only concerned with her outcome and if they need to negotiate again he may feel the need to be a lot more manipulative or aggressive in his style.

Fair or tough, soft or aggressive – the way you behave at negotiations is what people will be prepared for next time and will come prepared to deal with. So if we go back to Elizabeth's father, his aggressive approach meant that his suppliers and clients became extremely wary of him as a negotiator. What can happen is that the supplier or client feels that he has to match the toughness of the negotiating style which leads to their meetings becoming more and more contentious, until eventually they may break down altogether.

13

Three different outcomes

Most people are familiar with the three different outcomes that can result from negotiations. These can be expressed in simple terms as:

WIN–WIN
WIN–LOSE
LOSE–LOSE

WIN–WIN

This suggests that both sides get what they want. In reality it probably means that both sides feel satisfied with the outcome of the meeting. They may not have *everything* they initially asked for, but both have something. No one feels robbed or swindled.

WIN–LOSE

This is the classic first past the post scenario – if there is a winner, then by definition there has to be a loser. In negotiations this is often the approach that people take.

'I'm going for what I want and ****** the loser!'

or

> 'Our case is fair and their case is unfair so right is on our side and .we are not giving up until they give us what we want.'

WIN–LOSE is the classic starting position for many industrial and international disputes.

LOSE–LOSE

If both parties are determined not to let the other one win, they can both end up not achieving their objective. It can often happen when both parties go in with a WIN–LOSE approach and narrow desired outcomes, both determined not to give way. LOSE–LOSE can also be an attitude taken by both parties in a dispute.

> 'If we can't get what we want we are going to make jolly sure that they don't get what they want either.'

or

> 'She is obviously not going to give me what I want, so I am going to make it as painful and expensive as possible for her.'

These labels, WIN–WIN, WIN–LOSE and LOSE–LOSE are applicable both to the *approach* taken to the negotiation and to the *outcome* of the negotiation. The link that negotiators may fail to make is that the outcome is usually affected by the approach. If you start with a WIN–WIN approach, the outcome is far more likely to be WIN–WIN. If you start with a WIN–LOSE or LOSE–LOSE approach, the outcome will almost certainly reflect that.

Getting to WIN–WIN

There are a number of points which can help you to develop a WIN–WIN approach.

1 Separate the personality from the problem
2 Widen your horizons. Do not assume there is only one solution.
3 Look for a solution, not a battle.
4 Set it up to be constructive.

SEPARATE THE PERSONALITY FROM THE PROBLEM

Maybe you have negotiated with this person before and you know that he is a rat and that you really wouldn't want to pass the time of day with him, given the option. Last time you negotiated with him he was very unpleasant and was unwilling to give way on any of the issues which you regarded as important.

Forget it. Start again. Look at the problem rather than at the person who is coming to you with the problem. Your challenge is how to solve the problem in a way satisfactory to both of you, not how to sabotage the aspirations and career of the slimeball sitting opposite to you.

WIDEN YOUR HORIZONS. DO NOT ASSUME THERE IS ONLY ONE SOLUTION

The idea that there is one cake to be shared out between two people can limit the problem-solving capacity of otherwise brilliant negotiators. People get into the habit of thinking of one best solution, or a range of solutions which incorporates a fixed number of variables.

Take two children arguing about who should have the last two cakes on a plate. Even though there are two cakes, they naturally want the same one. Their view of the world is restricted to the two cakes. If they are canny children, they might see the option of cutting each cake in half and sharing both of them. But there are other options. The size of the plate of cakes can be increased metaphorically. If one child has the choice today, perhaps the other could have the choice tomorrow – so an extra element has been thrown into the equation.

If two people cannot agree on the price one of them should pay for some goods the other one wants to sell, the size of the cake can be increased by bringing in considerations such as discount for prompt delivery or penalties for late delivery, credit agreements or cash on the nail.

LOOK FOR A SOLUTION, NOT A BATTLE

Approaching a negotiation with the outlook that there is a problem to be solved rather than a battle to be won can have a startling effect on the process. People become locked in to thinking about negotiating as a process of winning as many points as they can while giving away as little as possible. (Obviously you don't want to give away too much without receiving something in exchange, and the tactic of trying to have some equity in how much is exchanged and getting something for what you give is discussed in Chapter 7.)

If you go into a negotiation thinking along the lines of 'fighting your corner' or 'making sure you get as much of the cake as you can', you are beginning to see yourself as one protagonist with the others involved as rival protagonists. This can set the scene for a WIN–LOSE approach.

If instead you see yourself and the others involved as equally interested parties, all needing a solution to a common problem, then you are moving towards a WIN–WIN approach. If each person or group involved has different needs, then their initial perception of the best way

15

to solve the problem may be different, but if both groups work towards a solution rather than a victory, everyone has a better chance of achieving more of what they need.

Take the game of Monopoly as an example. In this game, everyone tries to get as much property as they can, so that they can collect rent from the other players and eventually bankrupt them, thus causing them to lose the game. It would be possible to find a solution to Monopoly where all the players would be allocated property of roughly equal value, or devise a system of rebates for the less well off, so that all the players could continue playing (probably for much longer than they would want to!).

Monopoly is a game and the objective is to win the game. In real life, many people treat negotiations like a game, with their objective being to win. However, it may be more appropriate in real life to look for the solution, thus enabling all the players to achieve a more equitable outcome and continue operating effectively.

Many negotiators who do start with the idea of achieving a compromise struggle towards that compromise, trying to achieve the best result for themselves in what they know is a difficult area, rather than looking at the situation as two people or groups each with a problem which needs to be solved. It may be that some of the problem is caused by the other person or group, or the answer to the problem lies within the other group's control. Let's look at an example.

16

Frances, Anne and Jake work in the publishing department of a tourist board. Leaflets and posters are produced all through the year and these are distributed to the board's offices and to any members of the public who make enquiries.

Frances provides the artwork and photographs for the publicity material. She has to work closely with Jake who writes the copy, and Anne who is responsible for the finished article. They have to agree a deadline for the production of each leaflet. Each time, Frances has a battle with Anne about the deadline. It seems to Frances as if Anne wants the artwork to be completed yesterday, and Anne cannot understand why Frances is always late with the artwork, whereas Jake seems to be able to finish the copy in plenty of time.

Frances and Anne each approach the negotiation about when the deadline is to be with a huge and yawning gap between them, and eventually come to an agreement somewhere in the middle with neither of them satisfied.

If we look at it from the angle of each of them having a problem to solve it begins to look slightly different.

Frances's problem is that she has to provide both good quality drawings and photographs which illustrate the copy. It is difficult to know what to provide until she has some idea of what is included in the copy. Although Jake gives her a rough idea of what the copy will include and she can get together a portfolio of artwork which might be suitable, it is not until she sees the finished work that she can choose the best match. In some cases, it might mean altering a drawing or taking another photograph so that the copy can be illustrated to its best advantage.

Anne's problem is that she has to have the brochures or leaflets available for use by a certain date. She needs to have the finished article to give to the printers in good time, in case of delays or problems there. Sometimes the printers are not helpful about rush jobs. Sometimes there are a lot of mistakes in the proofs which need to be corrected.

In the past, Anne and Frances have always negotiated and compromised about time. Anne's problem has dominated the discussions and Frances has seen her own problem in terms of time also – Anne never lets her have enough to do the job properly.

If, instead of initially trying to squeeze more time out of each other, they were to look at each other's problem, both might discover a different perspective and be able to work together towards a constructive solution. For example, they might need to look at the way they schedule jobs, so that Jake's copy is available earlier in the scheduled programme of events. (This would also have the benefit of preventing some battles between Frances and Jake.) Or it might be possible to negotiate a different arrangement with the printers about when and how they incorporate the artwork.

17

Whatever the solution agreed, both parties will have a clearer idea of what lies behind the position the other is taking, which will lead future negotiations to be conducted with more of a problem-solving approach.

SET IT UP TO BE CONSTRUCTIVE

How can you do this? How can you get the negotiation off the ground so that the atmosphere from the start is constructive and positive? So that you seem to be helping each other to achieve what you want rather than battling for what you can both get?

Step 1 At the beginning of the meeting, summarise its purpose in positive terms. Why are you both there?

> 'We're meeting today to come to an agreement about new levels of pay/ how much maintenance is paid/ where we go on holiday/ the deadline for this piece of work/ etc.'

Avoid words like 'try to (come to an agreement)'. Sound as if coming to an agreement is a foregone conclusion.

Step 2 Make it obvious that you are taking a problem-solving approach.
Ask questions about their requirements in a way which shows that

you appreciate that they have a right to their wants, opinions and demands. Tell them how this causes you a problem and wonder aloud how you might begin to solve the problem.

'You say you need to have a firm date now, can I just check how vital that is to the programme?'

'You say that x will not be possible at this stage. My problem is that it will be very difficult to obtain y without x. I wonder if there is another way around this?'

Step 3 Involve them in the process of reaching a conclusion.

This isn't just your problem, it's a joint problem. Include them as partners in solving the problem you both face. Use phrases which involve the word 'we'. 'How can we . . .', 'Our problem seems to be . . .' or 'If we approach this . . .'. Ask them how they think the problem can be solved to the best advantage of both of you.

Step 4 Show your willingness to accept the other person's point of view.

Don't just use empathy, let them see that you are using it. Use phrases like: 'I can see . . .', 'You obviously feel strongly . . .', or 'It sounds as if . . .'.

Does WIN–LOSE ever become a realistic approach?

There may of course be situations where a win–win outcome is not appropriate. In May 1993 a gunman took six small girls and their teacher as hostages, in a French classroom. His ransom demands included millions of francs and a getaway vehicle. It would have been inappropriate to have let the gunman win even part of his outcome as to do so might have encouraged others to plan similar crimes.

However, the *approach* taken by the French police was a win–win approach. They brought some of the money and the vehicle he had demanded. They met his requests for food, a video camera etc. They stopped using this approach however when they were unable to negotiate with his final demand – to take a young child with him. The offer of one child's father was rejected. At this point their approach changed and they stopped even seeming to negotiate with the gunman's demands. At some point the gunman fell asleep (drugged perhaps) and the police, who had smuggled in a hidden camera with some food, were able to storm the building. The gunman was shot dead.

In this case, the gunman had to be seen to lose. If he had continued to negotiate, and had agreed to release the children in exchange for an adult, the situation might have continued longer and ended differently, but the outcome must have been the same – governments can not allow terrorism to be rewarded. So their reaction when hijackers take over aircraft, or Saddam Hussein uses a plane load of people as 'Human Shields' has to be a tough one.

There may be issues in your life and work which are so important that you have to win and be seen to win. Situations where you may need to exercise your right to refuse to negotiate. Let us hope they are slightly less traumatic and life threatening than the examples I have given here.

LOSE–LOSE

'Win–win is all very well if you both play by the same rules, but some of the people I negotiate with have never heard of it. They always play win–lose – and if they don't win, then they make sure that it's lose–lose all round.' Why do people take a LOSE–LOSE approach? Two of the most common reasons are:

1 They started out with a WIN–LOSE approach and they are not prepared to move.
2 They feel they are losing anyway, so they want to make sure the other people involved don't win.

19

REFUSAL TO MOVE

What if despite your best efforts, your problem solving win–win approach falls on deaf ears, and the person with whom you are negotiating sticks firmly to a win–lose position. One of the reasons they may be determined to win is that 'losing', i.e. giving away more than they want to or not getting as much as they would like, would entail losing face – losing credibility in the eyes of their colleagues, family, or even their opponent. It doesn't even have to be a real loss of face – if a person believes that they will lose credibility by a certain action, that is usually enough.

Help them to save face

In April 1993, many workers in East Germany went on strike, causing their employers to lose hundreds of thousands of pounds in lost production. They went on strike because their employers went back on an agreement to bring wages in East Germany up to the same levels as in West Germany. The employers said that they could not afford to pay what would have been a 26 per cent increase because they were using all their capital and profit to develop the industries. Bringing wages into line as had been agreed would have meant that the industries would have to close.

This was a classic LOSE–LOSE case. The workers were losing pay, the organisations were losing hundreds of thousands of pounds in lost production. The longer the strike went on, the more money the industries lost, so the more likely they were to go out of business, thus causing their striking workers to join the ranks of the unemployed.

For the main union involved, the problem seemed to be as much a matter of principle as of money. They had agreed contracts with the industries involved that would bring eastern wages to western levels by 1994. If this did not happen, the union were concerned that they would lose credibility and labour contracts would cease to have any meaning.

The dispute was finally settled with a smaller pay increase than the original demand, but *with a new date for bringing parity to eastern wages*. This was a face saving exercise, for both sides could now claim that they had achieved some sort of victory.

FEELING LIKE A LOSER

When people feel that they are losing in one way or another, a natural reaction is to try to prevent the other person from winning too much.

A good example of this is the acrimony which seems to accompany many divorce cases. Perhaps one partner feels hard done by, for a variety of reasons. They may feel somewhat vindictive towards the other partner. In these circumstances, they may try to get as much as possible out of the other partner *even if they do not really want or need it*. The aim is to maximise pain and distress for the other person to make up for the pain and distress they have caused.

This reaction is not restricted to divorce. It can happen in the home, office, factory, building site. When one or more people aim to cause as many problems for each other as possible, for whatever reason, the likely outcome will be LOSE–LOSE.

Negotiating with a confirmed WIN–LOSER or LOSE–LOSER

On occasions, however much you adopt a WIN–WIN approach and use all the techniques and tactics we have discussed in this chapter to encourage your opposite number to adopt a WIN–WIN approach, you may come across someone who is determined to take a WIN–LOSE or LOSE–LOSE approach. This can be an extremely irritating, frustrating and unproductive experience. What can you do about it?

Suspend irritation

You may find that you become irritated with their attitude. This can be a

20

problem because the irritation can begin to affect your ability to react rationally. Defuse your irritation by acknowledging that you feel it. Becoming consciously aware of the fact that you are irritated is the first step towards being able to put it on one side. Mentally parcel up your irritation and put it aside to be let out later in a safe place, then focus your energy on consciously practising your skills, such as using questions to explore the facts further.

Accept their attitude

If you can't change their attitude, accept that this is the approach they are going to take. The next step is to sort out how you will manage the situation. Remember that all behaviour has a positive intention. Even when people seem to be behaving in a totally antisocial and amoral way, there will be a positive basis for their behaviour. It may only be that it makes them feel that they have achieved something, or been noticed, but the positive intention is there.

So what might be the positive intention behind the insistence of your fellow negotiator to persist in a WIN–LOSE or LOSE–LOSE approach? If you can gain some insight into this, you may be able to modify your approach to give them what they need, which may then mean that they are able to take a less belligerent attitude. Here is an example of how one manager used a problem-solving approach to resolve a potential dispute, to the satisfaction of all parties involved.

21

Sandra was the manager of a number of products for a service organisation. She was asked to move into a new department, and there took over a major product from Simon who was moving onto a new team. The handover of Simon's product (Product X) took some time as there was a lot to learn, Simon was very protective of the way it had been developed and was concerned that the person who inherited it should be as expert and committed as himself.

Once Sandra was comfortable with Product X, her manager asked her to be involved with, then to manage the team responsible for developing, a related and more advanced product (Project W).

By this time, Simon had moved on. Sandra was now the acknowledged expert on the area which product X and product W covered. She was capable and efficient and managing both tasks well. The particular field was one in which there was a lot of interest, and within eighteen months of Sandra taking over product X, she had three staff who had joined her to work on it. She was asked by her manager to take on the responsibility for setting up and developing a third product, different from but closely related to the two she was currently managing (Project Z). At this stage, a number of undercurrents of dissatisfaction began to be felt within the department. Some of the people who worked with Sandra began to feel that she had altogether too much power. She was managing a major money earner in product X and had been asked to take responsibility for two other potential high status products in projects W and Z.

Alison, who worked for Sandra, was particularly dissatisfied. She felt that she had the capability and seniority to be managing one of these products, rather than just working on all three. Chamika did not particularly want a whole product to manage, but wanted to be responsible for something. Colin had recently joined and was content to carry on working on everything for the time being.

Sandra felt a bit hurt by the comments she was hearing. She had done a good and competent job in successfully taking over and developing a difficult and sensitive product which she was managing well. She was in the process of developing related products which were not by any means as well established or in demand as the product X. A meeting had been called by the departmental manager at which everyone was to have their say. Sandra knew that if she said that she wanted to keep the status quo as it was, she would have the backing of her manager. She also knew that doing so would increase the level of dissatisfaction amongst her staff. Alison particularly was spoiling for a fight.

Sandra decided that there were three issues of equal importance to her.

1 To ensure that the product was kept up to standard.

2 To ensure that customer needs were met.

3 To keep good relations with her colleagues.

These were of more importance than keeping responsibility for all the products. She decided to take a problem-solving approach, although she knew from comments made by others that Alison was determined to win control of one of the three products. She went to the meeting and was able to remain calm and even-tempered, despite some unpleasant and cutting remarks made by Alison.

Sandra asked everyone in the meeting to say what they wanted in terms of responsibility. She then put her views forward, in essence that while she would like to keep the responsibility she had at present, she also wanted to ensure that as many people as possible had the responsibility they wanted. She asked a lot of questions and was able to deal with antagonism from Alison calmly. They came to the following arrangement: Alison would be responsible for the day-to-day running of product X, with Sandra keeping nominal responsibility for a six-month handover period. Chamika would share some of the responsibility with Alison in that she would be responsible for a particular aspect of the product. Sandra would continue to carry complete responsibility for developing products W and Z, with everyone continuing to work on them. After six months, if all went well, Alison would officially manage product X, with Chamika keeping responsibility for her particular area.

So what made Sandra feel that this had been a WIN-WIN outcome? Although she had not kept responsibility for product X, for which she felt a great fondness and with which she was sorry to part, she felt that she had won good working relationships with her colleagues. She had achieved the concession of what was effectively a six-month handover period, so that she would be sure that Alison was comfortable and competent in handling this difficult and high profile product. She felt that everyone had come away from the meeting with something of what they wanted.

She was particularly pleased about this because she felt that when the meeting started, she had been the only one there with a WIN–WIN approach. Everyone else had been determined to fight their corner and gain as much as they could. Sandra felt that she had been prepared to take a problem-solving approach, separating the problem from all the personal antagonisms and emotions which were present, and being able to put aside her own feelings in the interests of achieving a solution acceptable to everyone.

Sandra was looking back at these events eight months after they had happened. Alison had taken full responsibility for product X by now, and although there were things which Sandra would have done differently had she still been in charge, product X was being managed satisfactorily. Chamika was happy with her responsibility and Colin was becoming more confident and playing a fuller part in the team. Sandra was involved in a number of smaller products, just as exciting and challenging, though not as major or high profile as product X, as well as keeping responsibility for products W and Z.

23

SUMMARY

- It is unlikely that many of the people with whom you start negotiating will start off with a problem-solving approach. Most people are so brainwashed into believing that negotiating is about winning that it takes a little while to get out of the habit.

- Taking the lead in using a problem-solving approach often has the effect of carrying the others in the negotiation along with you, changing their approach to the problem and causing them to see the situation in a different light.

Key points to remember

1 You will probably have to live or work with that person again.
2 The other person involved has wants, needs and a desired outcome for this negotiation.
3 Your behaviour now will set up expectations for the future.

Steps in using the problem-solving approach to achieve a WIN–WIN result

1 Separate the personality from the problem.
2 Widen your horizons. Don't assume there is only one solution.

3 Look for a solution, not a battle.

4 Set up the meeting to be constructive by:
   (a) summarising the purpose of the meeting
   (b) making it obvious you are taking the problem-solving approach
   (c) involving them in the process of reaching a conclusion
   (d) showing your willingness to accept their point of view.

5 If others are taking a WIN–LOSE or LOSE–LOSE approach:
   (a) help them save face
   (b) put your irritation away in a corner for later
   (c) acknowledge the positive intention behind the action.

3

Preparing to think on your feet

Preparation is the cornerstone for thinking on your feet in negotiations. Think back to some of the negotiations, formal or casual in which you have been involved, when you have been able to react quickly and effectively. The chances are that those were the occasions where you knew a great deal about the background and also the subject matter. You may have known your opposition fairly well and had a good idea of their investment and commitment to the subject. You were probably well aware of, and comfortable with, the balance of power between the two of you.

The times when thinking on your feet is not as easy are those when you are caught on the hop and haven't had time even to think about what you think! Someone comes up with a proposal completely out of the blue. You haven't had time to consider what the proposal means to you or your department. You don't know what might underlie their proposal, their motivations, their hidden agendas. You haven't had time to think about how balanced the swap might be, or how the outcome will affect you. Some people thrive on the rush of adrenalin they get when under this sort of pressure. Other people don't! Neither is it easy to think on your feet if you go into a negotiation overconfidently, so that you don't have enough knowledge of the situation and you haven't thought clearly enough about what you want to achieve. It is easy occasionally to think that you know your subject so well that you don't need to do any special preparation. This is one that you can handle off the top of your head. A problem may arise if the person with whom you are to negotiate *has* prepared properly. You may find that although you know the subject well, you are not prepared enough to be sure whether their proposal or request would be a good or a reasonable deal for you.

This chapter looks at the conventional and some less conventional approaches to preparing yourself to react quickly and effectively once you have entered the fray.

Foundations for thinking on your feet

Table 3.1 Thinking and preparation

Thinking about you	Thinking about them
Know your desired outcome	What might they want?
Know what you don't want	What might their limits be?
Know your limits	What might they be prepared to bargain with?
Know your bargaining counters	
Know your strengths and weaknesses	What are their strengths and weaknesses?
Know your ideal, realistic and fallback positions	What might their ideal, realistic and fallback position be?
Be aware of the balance of power	How much power do they have compared to me?

KNOW YOUR DESIRED OUTCOME

'If you don't know where you're going, you're likely to end up someplace else.'

This very irritating phrase is true to a certain extent in preparing for successful negotiations. However, if you know too certainly where you're going, and aim to get there come what may, the place you're going may turn out to be not as good as you thought it would be. There might have been other more attractive places which would have been even better if you had given yourself a chance to consider them. The converse to our irritating phrase could be:

'If you know where you're going so firmly that you're not prepared to go anywhere else, you may end up going nowhere at all.'

Any standard text on negotiating will tell you that you need to know your desired outcome before you start if you are going to have any chance of successfully getting what you want. This is true. It is important to know what you want. Sometimes, your desired outcome will be obvious and clear cut; at other times it may be a little more nebulous or obscure. There may be occasions where it may seem difficult to *really* know what you want. At other times, you may think you know what you want, then on reflection begin to wonder if another outcome would have been just as good or possibly even better.

Outcomes need to be specific, but not narrow. You need to know what it is you want without being vague about it, but if the outcome is too limited, it may restrict your means of achieving it.

So how do you decide on your desired outcome? How can you ensure that your desired outcome is specific, but not restricted?

FOUR STEPS TOWARDS DECIDING A DESIRED OUTCOME

1 Know what you want to achieve.
2 Think in the wider sense.
3 Know why you want it.
4 Make sure your outcome is positive.

KNOW WHAT YOU WANT TO ACHIEVE

What could happen if you began to negotiate without having any idea of what you wanted to gain?

(a) You could come away with a lot of gifts – if you didn't know what you wanted, anything you got would be a gift.
(b) You could be robbed – you could end up giving away valuable items while receiving concessions of little value to you.

So you need to have a clear idea about what you want at the end. But you need to be careful here – if your idea is too firmly fixed and not even slightly adjustable then you may be doing yourself a disfavour. If you are very thirsty and badly want a drink of water but the only thing available is lemonade, rejecting the lemonade because it is not water may not be in your best interests.

THINK IN THE WIDER SENSE

Thinking in the wider sense about your outcome means thinking about the end result you want to achieve rather than a specific goal. Broadening your thinking in this way can help you to find other ways to achieve your desired outcome. There are two questions you can ask yourself in order to think in the wider sense about your outcome.

(a) What would happen if I didn't achieve my desired outcome?
(b) Is there only one way to arrive at my desired outcome?

(a) What would happen if I didn't achieve my outcome?
What would you do if you did not achieve the outcome? What would be the worst thing that could happen? Perhaps your end result is to quench your thirst. If you didn't achieve your outcome, you'd carry on being thirsty, and depending on your environment this may or may not be

27

important. Perhaps the worst that could happen is that you would be very uncomfortable for another half an hour. But if you were stranded in the desert, you might die from dehydration.

When you begin to think like this, i.e. your end result outcome is to quench your thirst, you may find that there are a number of ways of achieving the result you want. Just as when you go on a journey to a specific destination, there are a number of ways of getting there, in a negotiation, there is likely to be more than one way of achieving your outcome.

(b) Is there only one way to arrive at my desired outcome?
When you plan a journey to a specific destination, there may be one logical and obvious way to go. However, if for one reason or another, it's not easy to use that route – maybe there are roadworks on the motorway or that stretch of road becomes very congested at a particular time of day – then there are other ways you can go which might take a little longer or a little more skill in navigating. The end result is that you get where you want to go.

KNOW WHY YOU WANT IT

Look behind your reason for wanting your outcome. Let us imagine that your outcome is to go to France for your holiday this year. You have to negotiate this with your holiday partner. Before you start trying to influence your partner towards France, think about what's behind your outcome. Do you want to go to France on holiday because

(a) you want to eat gourmet food?

(b) you want lots of cheap wine to drink?

(c) you want to see particular sights and sounds unique to France?

(d) you want to practise speaking French?

(e) it's fairly cheap to get there?

(f) you like the French way of life?

(g) you've always had a nice time there in the past?

(h) you've never been anywhere else on holiday and you don't like change?

(i) the weather is usually better than in Britain?

Knowing *what your reasons are* for wanting to go to France may help you to achieve your hidden outcome. These may not even be the reasons of which you are consciously aware , but may be those which are underneath the outcome you have stated to yourself.

Suppose that you normally go on holiday with three others. Your holiday companions have become bored with France because they have been there for the last ten years. They have come to a consensus that they want to go somewhere else, but two of them have no strong views about where it should be, the third wants to go somewhere a bit more exotic. Looking at your reasons for wanting to go to France may help you to come to an agreement about where to go which, although it may not be France, may give you some of the criteria you want. For example, if your main reason for going to France is to practise your French, there may be other places in the world which would offer you that opportunity – Martinique for example, or parts of Canada. If your main reason is lots of cheap wine, Spain or Portugal may do just as well.

If there are a number of very good reasons for sticking to France as a destination, perhaps you could agree to go to Corsica, where danger of bandits might make it feel a bit more exotic for your companions!

So before you decide on your objective, think about what you want to achieve, what is behind what you want. Is there more than one way of achieving your desired outcome, or do you truly have a very narrow goal?

29

MAKE SURE YOUR OUTCOME IS POSITIVE

Sometimes when people state their desired outcomes, they emerge in a negative form. The individuals know what they don't want. They may not want to work for that organisation, not make a fool of themselves, not become ill etc.

It is hard to work towards something which you are avoiding! It is much easier to achieve an outcome which is stated in a positive way. There is an easy way of changing negative outcomes into positive ones by asking yourself one simple question. That's what you/I don't want, what do you/I want?

Here are some examples of outcomes stated in a negative way, which can be changed into positive outcomes by asking that question.

1 'I want to avoid dealing with that man ever again.'

   That's what I don't want. What do I want?

   'I want to deal with people who negotiate with integrity.'

2 'I don't want to work on this project.'

   That's what you don't want. What do you want?

   'I want to work on projects which are relevant/interesting/fulfilling/ etc.'

Asking this question 'That's what you don't want. What do you want?' can be a very powerful way of helping yourself to clarify what it is you do want to achieve.

KNOW YOUR PRIORITIES

It is unusual for any negotiation to have one single issue to bargain about. If there is going to be give and take, it implies that you have something to give in order to be able to take. Even if it seems at first glance that there is one single concern, there is usually also some hidden matter involved.

Take the example of pay bargaining. The issue involved is how much more pay are the workers going to get from the management this year. It looks simple. It usually is not. Other concerns involved in this negotiation might be tying pay to productivity, having an agreement which lasts more than one year, or establishing a formula for future pay negotiations.

Once you know your overall objective, you need to break it down into its constituent parts, then prioritise those parts. If you were negotiating a pay settlement, which would be your first, second and third priorities? Which would be more important to you – to achieve the maximum increase this year, or to achieve a smaller increase now, with a guarantee of the same increase next year? Would you prefer to negotiate anew every year, or establish a formula? Would you be prepared to link pay to productivity if it gave you something you wanted in return? So the essential questions you must ask yourself here are: 'What is most important to me?' and 'What are the priorities in my desired outcome?'.

KNOW WHAT YOU DON'T WANT

Another useful question to ask yourself is: 'What would be totally unacceptable to me?'.

There may be some conditions or demands which you would not be prepared to accept at any price. It may be that it just would not be worth your while to continue if you had to go beyond a certain point, or that you would compromise your colleagues, honesty or integrity. Most people have a limit when they negotiate, but many people have not thought out this limit very carefully.

KNOW YOUR LIMITS

One of the most helpful things you can do when preparing to negotiate is to identify your limits. Knowing the point at which you are going to stop negotiating and say no, or get tough, or walk away, means that you can then begin to think about what you will do if that limit is reached.

Think also about what would happen if you didn't get what you wanted. What would be the best alternative? Fisher and Ury in *Getting to Yes*, (1981), identify a useful technique for preparing for negotiations. They suggest that you have a BATNA – a Best Alternative To a Negotiated Agreement. This means that you have something up your sleeve if you decide that your bottom limit is likely to be breached – it can give you the confidence to walk out.

When buying a car, a young couple went to a number of garages. In one garage they saw a car they liked. It met all their criteria of price, age, mileage. They decided to look further before buying it, and in the next garage they came across a car that was perfect for them. It was the right model, newer than they had hoped to get, it didn't have many miles on the clock and they even liked the colour. But – and it was a big But – it was more than they could afford to pay. They negotiated with the salesman. The negotiation went on for some time but the price the salesman was asking was above the top limit of the price they could afford. They went for a walk to think about it. They decided that the car they had seen in the previous garage would certainly meet their needs. Returning, they said to the salesman that they were unable to buy the car at that price, and that they had seen another car which they could afford and began to leave. To their astonishment, the salesman caught them up at the exit and said they could have the car at the price they had offered.

The young couple had a Best Alternative To a Negotiated Agreement. They knew that they could not go above a certain price and they were prepared to walk away from their ideal car because they could not negotiate a price that was acceptable. If they hadn't seen another car, their best alternative might have been to carry on having their old car repaired.

So if you are negotiating a promotion with your boss, what might be your BATNA if you don't get what you want? Look for a move? Put in fewer hours in the future?

If you are negotiating an important sale with a client and they don't want to buy at your price, what could be your BATNA? Sell at their price and make a reduced profit? Look for another client?

Your Best Alternative To a Negotiated Agreement will of course depend on your priorities. So this has to come a step behind thinking about outcomes and priorities.

IDEAL, REALISTIC AND FALLBACK POSITIONS

When you know what you want and what you don't want, and what is important to you, you can then begin to work out your ideal, realistic and fallback positions. These positions are a way of formalising your thinking about the outcomes you want to achieve and the limits you have. It's helpful to write them down.

What would be a good deal as far as you are concerned? What would be a satisfactory deal? What would be acceptable?

Your **ideal position** is what you would really like to have. This is what you want, and in an ideal world you will get it. When you begin the negotiation and state your position and what you want to achieve, you will be asking for the ideal position.

Your **realistic position** is what you might realistically expect to get, given that you have to negotiate with someone who is likely to want a different outcome to yours.

Your **fallback position** is your bottom line. This is the point beyond which you will not go, the point at which you stop negotiating and walk out.

However, there can be problems with ideal, realistic and fallback positions.

Problem one: pie in the sky

The **ideal position** is pie in the sky. Sometimes people think that if they ask for a wildly inflated idea of what they would like to have, they will have a better chance of getting what they really want. This doesn't always work, as all too often, the other side recognises its outrageousness, and counters with an equally outrageous first bid of their own. Your ideal position should have a chance of succeeding.

Problem two: unstretchy elastic

The **realistic position** is too high, too low, or too firm/unyielding. Your realistic position needs to be a range of positions, depending on what you want to achieve and why you want to achieve it. Sometimes if people have pie in the sky ideal positions, their realistic positions take over as ideal positions and they end up with a smaller range over which to bargain.

Problem three: stopping halfway down the bucket

The **fallback position** is too high. It is important when thinking about your fallback position to make sure that it really is your absolute bottom line. If you have your fallback position set too high, and find that you have to give in to pressure from the other party and go below it, you may lose credibility in their eyes if you have stated it was your bottom line. You may also damage your own self-esteem and begin to feel that you are a failure as a negotiator,or you may cause all sorts of problems for the people on whose behalf you have been negotiating.

Each year, the departments in a large, nationwide organisation need to make bids for their budget for the following year. Each year it is a bit of a lottery, as no one is quite sure how much money will be available in the budget. In 1991, a new departmental head who had no experience of this annual budgetary lottery took over the publications department. She decided that however much money they asked for, they were likely to get a lot less, so she asked for twice as much as the department thought they needed, thinking that this would allow her to negotiate down to a sum near to what was needed. To her amazement, the sum she first named was agreed without question. This meant that the department had twice as much money as it needed to operate over the following year. In fact it caused them a number of serious problems as they were severely underspent at the end of the year which meant that their bid for 1993 was compromised.

THE BARGAINING ARENA

Just as you have ideal, realistic and fallback positions, so will the person

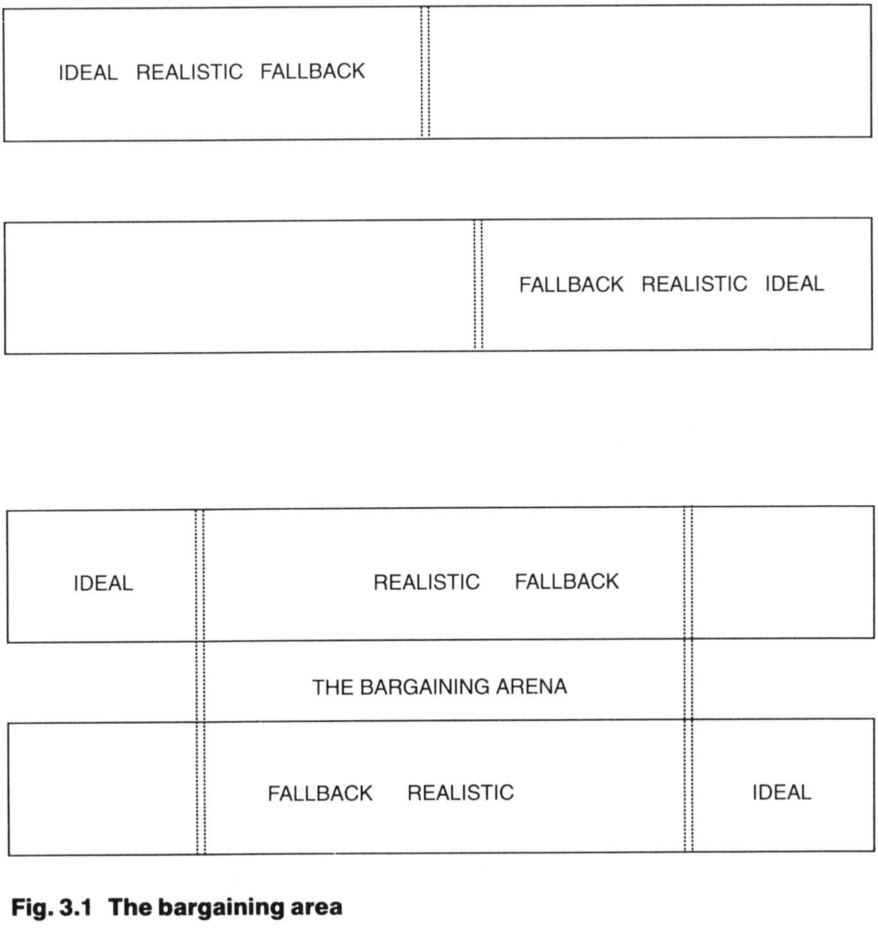

33

Fig. 3.1 The bargaining area

with whom you are negotiating. The bargaining arena is where your positions and their positions overlap. If they do not overlap at all, it is less likely that you will be able to achieve a settlement satisfactory to both sides. Once you have established your ideal, realistic and fallback positions, you can begin to prepare some of your strategies for the negotiation. One of the most important of these is the question:

WHAT CONCESSIONS CAN I MAKE?

Negotiating is about trading. If you are going to negotiate rather than dictate, you will need to be prepared to give something in order to get a settlement. You have already identified what you want to achieve. Now is the time to think about what you might be prepared to concede in order to achieve your outcome. This means going back to your list of priorities. Ask yourself:

(a) What must I have?

What is so important that I am not prepared to give way about it, even slightly?

(b) What is less important to me?

What do I have which I would prefer to keep intact but might be prepared to trade if I had to?

(c) What have I got to barter?

What do I have that isn't very important to me, or that I have a lot of, which I would be prepared to give away, in order to achieve what I want?

Think about negotiating bedtime with children. It might be important to you that they go to bed at 7.00, with their faces washed and their teeth cleaned. Assume they don't want to do that. They usually go to bed at 7.30. So you negotiate. If it's important to you that they get more sleep, but you have plenty of time to read them a story, you may negotiate with the offer of an extra bedtime story. If your priority is getting them out of the way because you have an important client coming to dinner, then you may offer the options of staying up later tomorrow or watching a cartoon on the video before going to bed. Your priorities will govern the things you are prepared to give way on and those which are non-negotiable.

KNOW YOUR STRENGTHS AND WEAKNESSES

The concessions you can make and the items you can trade depend on your strengths and weaknesses in that negotiation. Let's look at a situation familiar to most of us – moving house.

Adrian and Mary found a house they wanted in a suitable area. They sat down and worked out their strengths.

1 They were in a position to move quickly because they had sold their own house to a first time buyer, so they were not involved in a chain. Also, they had agreed in principle a loan from a building society.

2 They were not worried about whether or not they bought the curtains and carpets from the current owner. If they were included at a reasonable price, they were happy to live with them until they could replace them with ones of their own choice, or they would make do with second hand ones if not.

3 Although this was the house they had liked best in the area, there were other houses on the market which would do.

And their weaknesses?

1 Their main weakness could be in their first strength – they already had a buyer who might be pressurising them to move quickly.

2 Adrian had already started a new job in the area and was having to travel a long distance to and from work each day. They wanted to move soon.

35

These strengths and weaknesses compared to the unknown strengths and weaknesses of the vendors, might have some effect on whether or not the two parties were able to come to an agreement about price, moving date, etc which was satisfactory to everyone concerned. If we use the example of house purchase to compare the needs of two parties in a negotiation, we can see that what might be strengths in one instance might be weaknesses in another, depending on the circumstances.

So if, like Adrian and Mary, you have a strength which could also turn into a weakness, let the other party see your strength, but don't expose your weakness until you have to.

Negotiating is easy if you have similar needs

Depending on how overlapping your wants and needs might be, the more likely you are to achieve a settlement that is acceptable to both of you. If one of you wants to move quickly and the other wants to take his time selling his house, you are less likely to agree than if you both have similar needs in this respect.

KNOW THE BALANCE OF POWER

Be aware of the power you have in the particular situation where you are negotiating, making sure that you do not underestimate it. Have a look at the chapter on making the most of your power to ensure that you really do that. Then check that the person you are negotiating with has the power to make decisions. If someone is negotiating on behalf of another party, without having been given the power to make decisions on behalf of that party, negotiating can become a very drawn out and frustrating experience. They have to go and consult with their principal. This can mean not only delays, but new demands or suggestions when they return to the negotiation.

THINK ABOUT THEM

When you prepare, you don't just need to think about your own wants and needs, but also about what the wants and needs of the other party are likely to be. Put yourself in their shoes. If you were in their position, what would you want? Why might you want it? What might be the reasons behind you wanting this outcome? If you were in their shoes, what might be important to you? What might be your priorities, what might be the things about which you wouldn't be prepared to budge? What would be the worst possible outcome for you?

Take it a bit further, indulge in a bit of a dance. Step back into your own shoes and think about the various offers you might make to them, then back into their shoes to think about what it might mean to them. This is where you start a bit of a guessing game. Usually though, your guesses can be fairly educated ones. Your background knowledge of the situation will give you a pretty good starting point. You may have some knowledge of the person with whom you are negotiating. If you know them personally, you may have some knowledge of their usual style. If you know which department they come from, you may know the type of concession they will be looking for. If they come from another organisation, you may have a fairly clear idea of the outcome they will be looking for.

What issues are involved for them and where might their priorities be? What might their ideal, realistic and fallback positions be – what might be their BATNA? What are their strengths and weaknesses? What sort of things might they be prepared to trade? What might they lose – money, reputation, face? How important might it be to them to achieve a workable agreement?

Obviously, you are not going to be able to answer all these questions accurately, but even having thought about them and guessed about them means that you are better prepared to face the other party. One word of warning. *Let your guesses be hypotheses, be prepared for them to be wrong. Do not turn a guess into anything more concrete without some evidence.*

The more you know about what your adversary wants to achieve, the better placed you are to work out the sort of bargain you might be able to strike which will give them some of what they want while simultaneously getting most of what you want. All this may seem like a very long-winded, time consuming process. It is not. You should be able to do this groundwork in a very short time. The more used you become to thinking and preparing in this way, the more natural and easy it will become. It is important because being prepared for a negotiation means that you are more likely to be able to think on your feet – to react quickly and effectively to the ideas, questions, demands or suggestions made to you during the meeting.

Questions to ask yourself before you start

1 What do I want – what is my desired outcome?
2 What would be the worst that could happen if I did not achieve my desired outcome?
3 Is there more than one way to achieve my outcome?
4 Why do I want this outcome – what will having it do for me?
5 Is my outcome positive?
6 What don't I want and why don't I want it?
7 What are my limits – where will I stick?
8 What concessions can I make – what's important to me?
9 What are my strengths and weaknesses?
10 How can I show my strengths without exposing my weaknesses?
11 What would be a good deal?
12 What would be a satisfactory deal?
13 What would be an acceptable deal?
14 Do I have the power to negotiate with them?
15 Do they have the power to negotiate with me?
16 What do I think they want and why do they want it?
17 What issues are involved for them?
18 What are their strengths/weaknesses/ strategies likely to be?
19 How important is it to them, what would they lose if they didn't get an agreement?
20 How might any previous negotiation affect this one?
21 How might the custom and practice round here influence me or them?
22 What legal, factual or operational restraints need to be taken into account?

37

4

Making the most of your power

One of the most interesting and crucial elements involved in a negotiation is the balance of power between the various interests involved. If the two or more parties have different amounts of power and know it, there is already some inequality involved – they are not starting from the same place – its not fair!

When I run seminars on negotiating skills, one of the questions I ask the group is, 'What are the issues which influence the outcome of any negotiation?' One of the answers which always comes near the top of the list is POWER. Power is important in negotiations because:

1 People believe that it is important.
2 It can affect the ability of the negotiators to make decisions.
3 It can affect the outcome of the negotiation – the person with more power, perceived or actual, is likely to achieve more of what he wants.
4 It can affect whether a negotiation continues – the person with a lot of power can choose to impose her solution.

In organisations, people are overtly aware of power. It is something which has a bearing on their everyday behaviour, it influences who they talk to and deal with on a day-to-day basis. It may not be something which is talked about or referred to directly, but you know that if you are dealing with the Managing Director or Chairman of the Board, there may be differences in the way you approach them and the way you would approach a colleague at the same level, or a subordinate, with the same suggestion or request.

Outside of organisations too, power can be tangible at times. If you build an extension on your house, the building inspector has the power to come and inspect your property and tell you to put some more insulation here, or an extractor fan in the bathroom there. Officials in various government or local council offices have the infuriating power to block your request or withhold information which would be just what you needed if you only knew the right questions to ask. The police can signal you to pull over as you drive innocently along the road, and can ask you questions about where you have been or what you have been doing.

AWARENESS OF POWER

Power is something which we tend to think about in terms of how much power other people have. We tend to be much more aware of other people's power than our own. The awareness of power also depends to a certain extent on what you want. If you are a freelance consultant working for a management college, the power which various lecturers or directors have is of very little concern to you until they show some interest in employing you, or you want to influence them to employ you in some way.

The effects of the environment

In an environment where the norm is power based on status, usually used to coerce or reward, expertise is unlikely to have much influence. In environments where cooperation is the norm on which power is based, expertise, information and personal power are more valued. It used to be the case that in hospitals, the expert power of consultants was far more valued than the administrative power of the hospital administrators.

39

The effects of the situation

When you are trying to influence someone, such as when you are negotiating with them, you need to think about the relevance of your source of power. Power has to relate to the situation. The former Director of Public Prosecutions (D.P.P.), Sir Michael Green, had the power to make decisions about cases involving police and the courts at the very highest level. Yet when he was caught kerb crawling in a St Pancras street, the power he had as D.P.P. was of no use to him. The constable in the patrol car had more power *in that situation*.

Departmental and Regional managers have a lot more power than the secretaries or other clerical workers within the same organisation, but if one of them wants an appointment with the Chief Executive, his secretary will have a great deal of power to make that appointment or fail to find time in the diary. *In that situation* the secretary has more power than they do.

The management of a factory has power to hire and fire workers. If the workers decide to call a strike, they have a certain amount of power over the management, as loss of production means loss of profit. Individually, they have little power. In the situation where they join together to form a large group, they increase their power effectively enough to match or outweigh the power of management.

The effects of perception

'If you would be powerful, pretend to be powerful.'
Horne Tooke, 1736–1812

Remember that the amount of power you have will depend on the people on the receiving end of it and their perceptions of your power. It will also depend on the particular context in which you are operating. Power is only effective if people believe that you have it. It is *perceived* power rather than *actual* power which counts. Now in many cases, perceived and actual power do match up, but in cases where they don't, perceived power is usually more important.

It's not only how other people perceive your power that makes the difference – how you perceive it is of major significance. If you believe that your power is inferior to that of the person with whom you are negotiating, you are immediately putting yourself at a disadvantage. It is not uncommon to hear people say, 'He's holding all the cards', or 'She's got the advantage of me here'. Sometimes when you start thinking like this you can go on to convince yourself that you have no power at all in this situation.

40

Sources of power

Power comes from a number of sources, some of them external – those which other people or society gives us, and others of them internal – power which we give ourselves or allow ourselves to have. Let us have a look at some of these sources of power before doing a self-assessment of how much power you may have in different situations.

EXTERNAL POWER

External Power is the sort of power which comes from outside ourselves. French and Raven identified five different sources of power in 'The Bases of Social Power', 1959.

Legitimate power

This is the sort of power which comes from having a recognised position or authority. It is sometimes called Position Power. Legitimate power comes from being the manager of a department or section, and having authority to make certain decisions and take certain actions. It is the power a policeman has to ask to see your driving licence, the power of a bus conductor to ask you to leave the bus if you don't have the money to pay the fare.

It is power because people recognise the position you have as a legitimate one, and therefore recognise your right to do certain things. Legitimate power is limited to the areas where it is recognised as valid; for example, you may be a holy terror to the people who work for you, but step outside your area of authority and your power may well be non-existent.

Reward power

If you are able to give something to someone that they want, or withhold something they want, you have reward power. Every time a parent bribes a child they are using their reward power, every time a manager promotes a member of staff, a foreman allows someone to knock off early, or a rich nation sends aid to a poor nation. Having reward power means that you are able to give or withhold something that the recipient wants or expects. Reward power can be very effective and very useful; it can also backfire if used without careful thought.

Reward power needs to be relevant to the recipient. If your power to reward means that you are able to offer something which perhaps was of value in the past but is now readily available, or something which is valuable to most people but not to the person concerned, then it is useless. If a teacher has a large store of dinosaur stickers and gives them as a reward for good work, her reward power will be severely reduced when dinosaurs fall from favour and footballers, pop stars, or twenty-seven different types of roller skate become the latest rage.

41

Coercive power

If reward power is a parent bribing a child with a bar of chocolate, coercive power is the child threatening to scream all the way around the supermarket *unless* they are given a bar of chocolate. Having coercive power means being able to make threats about what will happen if your wishes/demands/wants are not met, *and having those threats believed.* The person on the end of the threat knows that you have something unpleasant up your sleeve which you will not hesitate to use if provoked. Again, the crucial element to coercive power is that whoever you are threatening *believes* that you have the means to carry out the threat you have just made.

Often, Reward power and Coercive power go hand in hand. though not always. Management have reward power, unions have coercive power. Parents have both reward and coercive power – as do children.

Anne Jackson is a working mother who regularly on a Friday night picks up her young daughter from the childminder and stops off at the supermarket on the way home. Five o'clock on a Friday is a busy time at the supermarket, it is crowded and the only safe place for a two-year-old child is in the seat of the trolley. Lucy doesn't like sitting in the trolley, she likes to help. Anne is usually tired by the end of the week, and her daughter is tired by the end of the day. The child is always a little grumpy when her mother first collects her: Anne often thinks that it is as if the child is trying to punish her for not being with her all day.

On one occasion, when Lucy was grizzling, Anne gave her a packet of Smarties to keep her quiet while she got the groceries in relative peace. The next time they went to the supermarket, Lucy wanted Smarties again. Anne refused, saying that she could have some after she had had her tea. At this, Lucy staged a full blown tantrum, which even those of you who are privileged not to have been on the receiving end of, have probably witnessed. Half-way round, Anne could stand it no longer and handed out the Smarties.

Smarties are now a regular feature of the Friday night shopping trip at the supermarket. They are no longer an example of Anne's reward power, but of Lucy's coercive power.

The same story could be repeated many times in hundreds of different guises – a reward which becomes seen as a right, with coercive power applied if it is not carried out.

The management of a biscuit factory unofficially allowed night shift workers to finish early when production targets were reached. Over time, workers ensured that production targets were always reached in time to allow them to finish about an hour before the shift officially ended. When a new night shift manager attempted to introduce higher production targets thus threatening the early finish, the workers threatened to strike.

Expert power

This is perhaps the most acceptable kind of power. Expert power is perceived as having been worked for: you only get expertise if you have experience or knowledge. It is the kind of power which is most likely to feel comfortable both to those who have the power and those who experience its use. Anyone who knows a lot more about a subject than all those around her has expert power. People are willing to accept it as valid. The amount of expert power you have depends on the people you are working with: an archaeologist among other archaeologists will have less expert power than an archaeologist consulted by a group of lay people. Expert power can also be intimidating; in the case of someone who has a lot of technical knowledge advising someone who does not.

You take your car to the garage for a service and the receptionist rings you mid-morning to say that there is something technical and complicated wrong with it which needs to be put right. She probably names the thing that is wrong with the engine, but your mind immediately edits out that information because it doesn't understand it. You need your car in order to make an important journey tomorrow. What do you do?

In this sort of situation, you are likely to feel powerless and helpless. You may feel that you have very little choice but to tell the garage to do the repairs, probably landing you with a much larger bill than you had bargained for. The expertise of the garage mechanic is more than a match for your power as a customer wielding the money, although it might be thought that in a situation where one has money to buy and the other has service to offer, the power lies with the buyer.

Referent or charismatic power

Some people have power just because of the sort of person they are. You may know someone at your place of work, or socially, who seems to be able to pull people along with her with very little effort. Usually they have something about them which other people admire or want to emulate. The middle aged of any generation are usually puzzled and amazed by the sort of power and influence which unkempt and badly dressed pop stars have over the young. Pop stars sometimes go on from having referent power to having position power – their record at the top of the charts, or reward power – the ability to give favours to fans.

43

Other kinds of power not identified by French and Raven but readily recognisable inside and outside of work are:

Connection power

This sort of power is to do with who you know, what influence you might be able to have in circles which matter. If you are friendly with or related to someone with power and influence, the people around you may believe you to have connection power; that you have the ear of the MD or the Chairman of the Board. Connection power has often been a way in which children followed their parents into the same profession – a well-thought-of worker has a word in the ear of the foreman, or a barrister puts in a good word for the son of a former schoolfriend.

Information power

The person who is perceived by others as having information which nobody else has, has information power. Often, people with legitimate power have information power, but it is also a form of power which can be held by those who have no formal power at all within an organisation. The managing director's secretary, who knows her whereabouts and the state of her diary, the messenger who always knows the latest gossip on what is going on in the boardroom. That person in your organisation who always seems to know before anyone else what is going on.

Of course information power has a more serious side. It belongs to those who know exactly how many people need to be made redundant, where and when. It belongs to those who know when critical changes in the organisation are to be made, and who is likely to be most affected by them. Once more, you don't actually need to have the information all of the time – you just need other people to believe that you have it.

Physical power

This is arguably the most basic sort of power – and perhaps the most obvious. It is used by countries to make war or threats of war, by individuals or gangs of thugs and hooligans terrorising neighbourhoods or the elderly, by parents over their small children. It is a very effective and can be a very intimidating kind of power. It is often, but not exclusively, used coercively. It can be used beneficially – for example a parent restraining a child from running on to the road, or a strong person assisting someone weaker to achieve an objective.

44

Negative power

Negative power is the power to stop things happening, to disrupt, to delay things. It is often used coercively, but can also be used in a passive way. When Gandhi started his Civil Disobedience campaign in 1930, to try to gain Independence from the British, he and the Indian peasants he led had no apparent power. Gandhi did not incite his followers to an uprising against the British. He asked them instead to disrupt the power of the Empire by negative means – sitting on railway lines to disrupt communications, refusing to cooperate with the Establishment.

Negative power is usually latent. It isn't apparent until someone begins to use it. For example, the person who opens and sorts the mail for an office has very little power. However, if there comes a day when she feels aggrieved for some reason and hides or wrongly distributes the mail, her negative power may have repercussions for the whole office.

A bus driver has very little overt power. Her negative power could be expressed by driving past a group at a bus stop on a rainy night because she was behind with her schedule, or because she had had a row with her boss or her partner perhaps.

MAKING THE MOST OF YOUR EXTERNAL POWER

1 Identify it by using the questionnaire at the end of the chapter.
2 Heighten your awareness of it. Admit to yourself that you have this sort of power.

3 Think about how you could use it to best advantage, how can you demonstrate that you know you possess that type of power.

4 Make sure that the other people in the situation know that you have the power.

5 Demonstrate your ability and willingness to use it, perhaps by reference to times you have done so in the past.

INTERNAL OR PERSONAL POWER

When we think about power, we tend to think about external power, the power of position, strength, rewards, punishments, expertise. One source of power we think far less about is our own internal power, the power we have inside ourselves.

The amount of internal power we have depends to a large extent on how powerful we *allow* ourselves to be. There are other labels for internal power, such as confidence, self-esteem, self-reliance. It can also come over as determination, conviction or a sense of purpose. Whatever the label for it, the amount of internal power you have will have an impact on the amount of power you are *seen* as having by others.

45

HOW WE LIMIT OUR OWN POWER

Many people limit their own power. They do it in two ways:

(a) By downgrading in their own eyes the amount of power they have.

(b) By effectively giving power away to other people by being more willing to legitimise and recognise power that other people have.

The interesting thing about power, is that it doesn't have to be used. The fact that people believe that someone has it is enough. While this can work in your favour if other people believe that you have power, it can also be a limiting factor on your power if you believe that other people have more than you. Even if others do have more power than you do, there is a tendency to credit them with more power than they actually have.

The chief executive of a software company has plenty of legitimate power. However, she has more power within the organisation than her position alone warrants. Because she is well aware of her own power, other people behave towards her in a way which legitimises and reinforces her power and diminishes their own.

Power and beliefs

The sort of beliefs we have about our own power and the power of other people can have a huge impact on how powerful we are.

Fiona and Alison both work for the same boss. During the course of one month, a particularly busy period in that department, both Fiona and Alison needed to take two days off, for personal reasons. When Fiona went to her manager, she had little expectation that she would be able to have the time she needed. She knew that he had the power to make this decision and she felt that she was in a very poor position to ask for the time, as it was a busy period, she felt embarrassed and awkward about asking. When Alison went, she was also aware of the manager's power to make the decision. However, she was also aware of her own worth as a valuable member of staff and was confident of her ability to convince her boss that she could make up the work when she returned.

Neither of these women had a better reason than the other to be given the leave. Both were equally vital to the efficient functioning of the department. The fact that the manager refused the leave to Fiona and granted it to Alison, may have been based on a number of causes, but was certainly to a large extent the consequence of how powerful each woman had felt in that situation.

For some people the thought of negotiating engenders feelings of nervousness, or inadequacy or a general loss of confidence in their ability to do this part of their job excellently. It's not only at work that the thought of negotiating engenders these feelings. If person A knows that she has to come to an agreement with person B, about a subject to which they do not have a common approach, and that the subject is important enough for them to discuss it formally, person A may well feel nervous or lack confidence about her ability. Feelings can range through nervousness, anxiety, inadequacy, fear of failure, and a general lack of confidence. This is not something that they enjoy doing nor feel that they have any expertise to conduct.

FEELING MORE CONFIDENT – THE POWER OF BELIEFS

Where do these feelings come from? Why is it that in some situations we feel inadequate, we fear failure, we are sure that other people will be able to perform better than we can? Feelings spring from our beliefs about ourselves. Imagine your own power, confidence and ability to influence, as a bucketful of feelings. At the top of the bucket is a layer of self-confidence – the internal power you can use to increase your ability to influence. Below that is a layer of self-esteem, how positively you perceive yourself and your ability to deal with problems. Below that are the beliefs you have about yourself which have been built up and reinforced from childhood, through school and working life. Beliefs which have been engendered by other people's reactions to you, by the attitude of parents, peers, teachers, supervisors and by your own successes and failures.

Your beliefs about yourself affect your behaviour, which influences

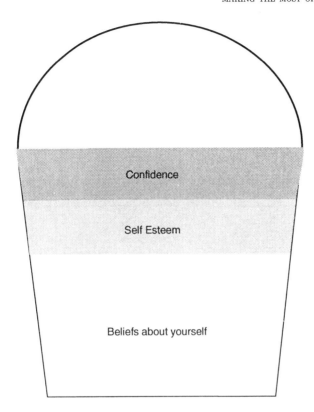

Confidence

Self Esteem

Beliefs about yourself

47

Fig. 4.1 The bucket of beliefs

other people's perception of you. This affects their behaviour towards you, which reinforces your belief about yourself. Figure 4.2 illustrates the situation as a circle of beliefs.

INCREASING YOUR PERSONAL POWER

There are ways in which you can increase your personal power:

- be aware of your power
- harness your inner voice
- think about the positive not the negative outcome
- remember they may need something from you.

Be aware of your power

Recognise and acknowledge the external power you have in each situation. There will be very few situations where you are absolutely powerless. Focus on successes you have had in the past, in similar

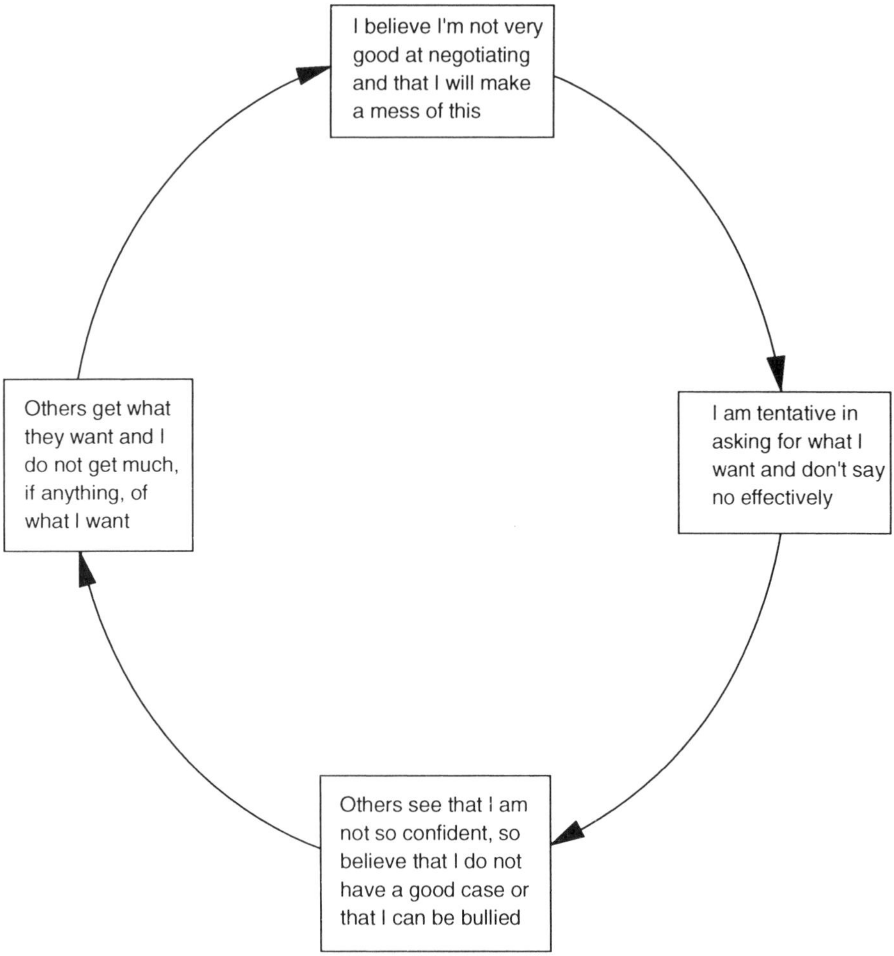

Fig. 4.2 The circle of beliefs

situations. It is easy to remember the times you messed things up – put those to the back of your mind and dredge to the surface the times you were successful and competent. You don't need to be modest, you are only reminding *yourself* about how good you are.

Be aware of what you have to offer. Do you have some skill, some knowledge, something which can add value to the problem, negotiation, or decision-making process?

Harness your inner voice

I expect you are familiar with your own inner voice – the one that says, 'You made a real mess of that; what were you expecting anyway, trying to take on something you should never have attempted in the first place?' We all have an inner voice. Sometimes it encourages us to go on and do something different, or congratulates us when we achieve something. More often it is a negative voice, pointing out all our faults and failings mercilessly, but failing to do the same for successes and achievements.

We all need a warning voice to ensure that we don't become over-confident, or do dangerous things, but if your warning voice becomes a discouraging, negative voice, check the reality of what it is saying. Negative voices often talk in absolutes: you always mess it up, you never act confidently, everyone will be criticising, you'll get it all wrong. A reality check allows you to put a rein on your inner voice and change the absolute into shades of grey. Do you really *always* mess it up?

You can turn your inner voice into an asset which will help you to feel less nervous and make your outcome more positive. Think of your inner voice as a supporter, cheering you on. Let it say something along these lines to you: 'You're going to make a success of this. You really know more about this than anyone else. You are the expert. You have a lot of experience in this subject. You are perfectly capable of negotiating with this person. You have done your preparation thoroughly and know you can cope. You've done far more difficult things than this in your life before. This may not be easy but you can do it well.'

Think about the positive, not negative outcome

Most people have had an experience about which they felt nervous. Having to give a vote of thanks to a speaker or make a presentation yourself, asking someone more senior than yourself to do something for you, presenting a report to a meeting. All these and many others are the sort of occasion which start the butterflies moving.

Before the event, it's all too easy to imagine what can go wrong. Sometimes our inner voice has a field day on these occasions: 'What if my voice dries up or I have a coughing fit. I'll probably forget what I want to say or I might drop my notes. What if my mind goes completely blank? Perhaps I'll get my words mixed up like that vicar who said Brides and Gownies instead of Guides and Brownies and everyone will laugh at me. I'm sure to go bright red and everyone will know that I'm nervous/embarrassed. I'm sure they will have a better case than I will. They've got far more experience than I have.' . . . and so on.

The problem with being only too well aware of what can go wrong, is that it can begin to drain your confidence. You may feel less sure that you have all the facts at your fingertips and begin to doubt your own ability to carry out the presentation or carry off the negotiations.

Think positive. Think 'I can do this. I have prepared, I have all the knowledge I need, there is every reason why I can look forward to a

49

successful outcome. It will go well . . .' and so on in that vein. It may sound implausible, but it works.

Remember they may need something from you

When you are negotiating, however powerful and strong the other party seems to be, remember that they would not be negotiating with you unless they wanted something from you. It may be money, time, knowlege, skill, or even more nebulous concepts such as cooperation, goodwill, or lack of opposition. Whatever it is, when you are negotiating, *you have some power.* If you have not identified what that power is or where it comes from, do so, because that is one way of increasing it.

Power is part of any negotiation. You can increase your chances of using the power you have at your disposal by acknowledging and being prepared to use your external power and by taking a good look at your beliefs and how they affect your behaviour and your internal power. Use the following questionnaire to identify your external power and increase your internal power.

Look at the situation

Remembering that power is relative to the *situation* you are in, and the people you are with, *apply these questions to each situation*, rather than using them as a blanket test. The questions are based in organisations, but can be applied to other groups.

1 Are you an expert on the subject?
2 Are you representing someone, or do you have an official position?
3 Do you have any inside knowledge?
4 Do you know anyone who might be able to influence the outcome?
5 Do you have the sort of personality which can charm ?
6 Can you apply any sanctions or other pressure?

IDENTIFY YOUR EXTERNAL SOURCES OF POWER

Legitimate or Position Power

1 Do you have formal and recognised authority in your role? (e.g., authority stated in your job description).
2 Do you have to give your approval before others can take action?
3 Do you have the formal right to take decisions?
4 Do you supervise other people?

Reward Power

1 Do you have control over valued resources in your organisation?
   (a) money?
   (b) promotion?
   (c) access to senior managers?
   (d) times of work?
   (e) holidays?
   (f) training opportunities and budgets?
   (g) expenses?
   (h) other perks of the job?
2 Are you able to reward people with praise for a job well done?

Coercive Power

1 Are you able to use your control over any of the resources mentioned for Reward Power as a sanction or punishment?
2 Does your position allow you to criticise or blame without challenge?

51

Expert Power

1 Do you have knowledge of a specialised subject or aspect of work?
2 Does it take a long time to learn to do your job?
3 Do you need a qualification to be able to practise your skill or knowledge?
4 Is someone with your skills and knowledge unusual in the organisation?
5 Is your specialised subject valued within the organisation?
6 How often are you consulted about your specialised area of skill?
7 Do more senior people consult you about your particular area of expertise?

Charismatic Power

1 Do people of the same status as you seem to do what you ask them to without you having to use too much pressure?
2 Do people seek you out for a social chat or for advice?
3 Do your subordinates do things for you cheerfully and willingly?
4 Are you popular?

Connection Power

1 Are you friendly with anyone who is perceived as powerful?

2 Do you know people who might use their influence on your behalf?

Information Power

1 Do you have access to valuable information before most other people in the organisation?

2 Do you have a network of people who keep you informed about what is going on?

3 Do you have specific information about potential changes or initiatives before other people?

4 Do others seek you out to find out the latest news or gossip?

Physical Power

1 Are you physically stronger than those around you?

2 Are you asked to help with physical tasks?

Negative Power

1 Do your actions have the capacity to make life uncomfortable for a particular group?

2 Can your lack of action have the capacity to make life uncomfortable for a particular group?

3 Can your behaviour disrupt life enough to make others want to negotiate with you?

4 Do you have the motivation and nerve to carry out disruptive or passive negative action?

5 Are you prepared to threaten to do so?

For each of the sections above, the more you answered 'Yes', the more of that type of power you have. You will probably find that in some situations, you may have legitimate power, whereas in others you have expert power or reward power. In a number of instances you may have more than one type of power.

INCREASE YOUR INTERNAL POWER

1 What beliefs do you have about yourself that are limiting your internal power?

2 What evidence can you find that these beliefs are not true?

3 Have you checked the reality of any negative messages you are giving yourself?

4 How can you turn your inner voice from a critic into a champion?

5 Have you started thinking positively about the outcome?

6 What do they want from you?

7 Are you giving them more power than they actually have?

Putting your case effectively

The first formal part of any negotiation is where you state your case, say what you hope to achieve and perhaps how you hope to achieve it. One of the basics of good negotiating, which is needed before your facility at bargaining or your tactical competence, is your ability to put your case effectively. The impression you make as a negotiator at this first stage will affect the other person's perceptions of you. These first impressions will form the foundation for their attitude towards you and may make it either more or less difficult for you to work with them effectively.

There are three key elements in putting your case effectively

- look and sound confident
- be assertive
- build rapport.

Look and sound confident

A confident image is useful in more ways than one. If you look confident

- people will believe that you *are* confident
- people will be more inclined to believe that you are competent
- and if other people treat you as competent, you will start to feel more confident yourself.

Whenever we meet someone for the first time we make instant judgements about them, and base our initial reactions on those judgements. Some of these judgements will be modified, a few quickly, and others over a period of time. Research by psychologists has suggested that:

55 per cent of the impression you make on other people will be governed by what they SEE. This includes colour, sex, appearance, posture, facial expressions, gestures, and clothing.

38 per cent of the impression you make will be governed by what they HEAR, including tone of voice, accent, speed and pitch of voice and clarity of speech.

7 per cent of the impression you make is governed by the WORDS you use.

So someone is far more likely to be influenced by how confident you look and sound than by the words you use. This suggests that however well you have prepared your case and researched theirs, however good your problem-solving techniques and negotiation skills might be, unless you also look and sound confident about what you are doing, you are going to have an uphill struggle to arrive at a satisfactory outcome.

DRESS FOR SUCCESS

There are probably not many people who would feel confident addressing a business meeting, if dressed in the clothes they wear to turn out the attic, or take the garden rubbish to the dump. Most people will have a range of clothes that they feel are appropriate to certain situations, and will feel more confident if they are dressed appropriately for the occasion.

There are some occasions which are not clear-cut and where you can make an effect on how confident you feel by the way you dress. I have a friend who deals with senior managers and board members every day and dresses in business suits to do so. Whenever she needs to go to her children's school however, she dresses far more casually. On one occasion, she was in dispute with the headmaster whom she felt was patronising her. On the next occasion of their meeting, she dressed in her 'work clothes'. She felt that the headmaster treated her with more respect on that occasion. It is difficult to know of course, who was affected by the clothes she was wearing – was the headmaster seeing her in a different light – or was she behaving differently because she felt more confident in tackling difficult situations in those clothes. Perhaps it was a mixture of the two.

Many books have been written about image and how to change your image by the clothes you wear. Clothing is definitely an important part of your image. Richard Branson, the proprietor of Virgin Atlantic is well known for his casual image of sweaters and casual trousers. In the dispute in 1992–3 between British Airways and Virgin Atlantic where Virgin Atlantic emerged a clear winner, Lord King, then Chief Executive of British Airways was heard to say that he would have taken Richard Branson more seriously if he had worn a suit!

Richard Branson is either rich enough, powerful enough or confident enough to feel comfortable with an image which does not always fit in to the *accepted* image of his surroundings. The majority of people however feel most comfortable if they are conforming to the image which is the norm for the particular surroundings they are in at the time. People who wear something startlingly different from the norm may well be trying to draw attention to themselves for one reason or another. Many teenagers seem to go through phases where first of all they are terrified of wearing something different from their peers, then wear what seem to

55

older generations to be startling and uncomfortable sets of clothing.

Choose an image with which you are comfortable and which makes you feel confident, then choose the clothes that will help you to fit that image. If you feel more confident wearing clothes that fit the norm of your surroundings, check to see what the norm is. If you feel more confident wearing clothes you feel comfortable in, and hang the rest of society, then do that!

PRACTICAL WAYS TO SOUND MORE CONFIDENT

Having made an initial judgement about you by the way you look, people will then confirm that judgement by the way you sound. You may not be able to do much about your accent, and you may not want to go to the trouble and expense of elocution classes to improve your tone and pitch. Let us have a look at what you can do which will help you to sound more confident.

1 Lower the pitch of your voice slightly. A lower pitched voice is more attractive and sounds more authoritative. You are probably aware from your own experience that when you are nervous, the pitch of your voice tends to get higher, so if you consciously lower it a tone, it will probably return to its normal pitch.

2 Hold up your head and say your words clearly and distinctly. You may have come across the lecturer who talks earnestly to his flip chart, the manager who addresses her notepad, and the children who speak to their food. In all cases, the impact of their words is lost in the flipchart, notepad or plate of spaghetti.

FEELING MORE CONFIDENT

Looking confident and sounding confident are two things that will help you to feel more confident. The third part of the set are your beliefs about yourself. These are explored more fully in the chapter on power. Your beliefs about yourself affect your behaviour, which affects other people's perception of you and this in turn affects their behaviour towards you. This may then affect your belief about yourself and if you believe that you will fail, then you are more likely to fail. Believing that you will succeed does not guarantee success, but brings success a lot closer. Help yourself to believe that you can succeed:

- be aware of your power
- be aware of your skills and knowledge
- think about the positive, not negative outcome
- be aware of what you have to offer.

Be assertive

Aggressive, passive or assertive approaches.

Appearing and sounding confident also involves the manner in which you put your case across. Many negotiators feel that unless they appear to be 'tough', they will be thought 'soft' and the other party in the negotiation will take advantage of them. In some cases, 'toughness' implies an aggressive approach.

AN AGGRESSIVE APPROACH

An aggressive approach is not always the one which gets the best results. What can be some of the positive and negative aspects of putting your case and reacting to proposals aggressively?

Positive
- You sometimes get your point pushed through
- People take notice of you
- You don't give in easily
- You show yourself as someone to be reckoned with

Negative
- You may make an unpleasant impression
- People may not want to work with you again
- You may antagonise people
- You may achieve what you want now, but harden people's attitude to you for the future
- Others may become aggressive, leading to stalemate, deadlock, conflict.

An aggressive approach tends to antagonise people and stimulate them to become aggressive themselves.

A PASSIVE APPROACH

If you do not take an aggressive approach, another option is to be accommodating and passive. If you are not confident about your case, or your power, or your ability to handle the situation, sometimes you may end up taking a passive approach – giving way to the other person. The 'soft' approach tends to imply giving way, being nice to people, saying you will do what they want or they can have what they want. There are some positive and negative aspects of the 'soft ' approach too:

Positive
- You appear to be conciliatory and pleasant

Negative
- You will gain very little of what you want

- By giving in this time, you may gain something next time
- It gets the whole business over with quickly

- You give the impression of being a soft touch – next time they'll come expecting even more from you
- You will feel less confident about yourself as a negotiator
- You may give away more than you can afford.

Between the tough and the soft approaches is the assertive approach. The word Assertive is often misinterpreted and used to mean aggressive. There are some big differences between aggressiveness and assertiveness. Let us look at the distinctions between them.

Aggressiveness implies two opposing parties, one of which must win. Assertiveness on the other hand, is about working together to achieve a joint solution.

Table 5.1 Aggressive or assertive

Aggressiveness	Assertiveness
Definition: Standing up for your rights in such a way that you disregard the rights of other people.	*Definition*: Standing up for your rights and paying attention to other people's rights.
Aim: To win. To achieve your objective regardless of anyone or anything else.	*Aim*: To achieve what you want while respecting what other people want and coming to a solution which will satisfy both.
Behaviour: Ignoring the needs, wants and opinions of other people.	*Behaviour*: Taking the needs, wants and opinions of others into account.
Saying what you want or need or think in inappropriate ways.	Saying what you want, need or think openly and directly.
Heavy emphasis on 'I'. What I want, need, think.	Asking others what they want, need or think.
Loud voice, abrupt tone, sharp questions to challenge rather than enquire.	Saying 'I' without heavy emphasis.
Interrupts frequently, doesn't listen.	Calm voice and tone, questions to enquire not challenge.

The popular image of assertiveness is getting what you need at all costs. In fact, this is aggressive behaviour, true assertiveness means getting what you want if at all possible, while being aware of other people's needs.

USING ASSERTIVENESS IN NEGOTIATIONS

Being in an assertive frame of mind can help you to feel confident and to put your case effectively. So how do you get there? Be aware of your rights in the situation.

Assertive Rights in negotiating

You have chosen or have been chosen to carry out this negotiation. Therefore, keep in mind that:

- You have the right to be there.
- You have the right to be treated respectfully.
- You have the right to ask for information.
- You have the right to say what you want, think and feel.
- You have the right to disagree.
- You have the right to change your mind.
- You have the right to be listened to.
- You have the right to think before reacting.

Assertiveness means a direct, open approach. It means saying what you want in a direct, open and clear way. *It does not necessarily mean spilling all the beans at once.*

Know what you want

It is much easier to be assertive when you know what you want. If you go to your manager to ask for more interesting work, it is much easier to be assertive if you have worked out beforehand exactly what it is you want to achieve.

Imogen worked for a building society. Her job was to wordprocess all the letters which went out from the branch to customers and to type all the manager's other correspondence and reports. Imogen enjoyed her job, but at the same time wanted some variety. She knew that she didn't want to be a wordprocessor operator for the rest of her life, and wanted a bit of challenge.

If Imogen had gone to her manager saying that she wanted a change, that she didn't want to spend all her time word processing, this story might have had a different ending. But she didn't. She thought before she went to see him, and decided that she would like to be able to work with customers at the counter. Because she knew that this might not be possible straight away because of existing staffing arrangements, she was able to put her request in a way which showed that she had thought through some of the problems and come up with some solutions. She was sure of what she wanted and what the objections might be, so she felt confident and was able to be assertive in stating what she wanted.

59

An assertive voice

The biggest difference between being aggressive and being assertive is not in what you say but in the way that you say it. For example the sentence 'I think we ought to do it this way', can be said aggressively, assertively or passively, entirely dependent on the tone of voice in which it is said, and the emphasis placed on the words.

'*I* think we ought to do it *this* way'

said in a loud voice, with heavy emphasis on the italicised words will be **aggressive**.

The same sentence said in a level voice, with slight emphasis on the italicised words would be **assertive**.

Said in a tone of voice quieter than those around without emphasis could be **passive** – it's unlikely that anyone would take much notice.

SAYING NO EFFECTIVELY

Any standard text on assertiveness will teach you to say no in a direct, honest and open way. When you are negotiating, you still need to be direct honest and open, but you may need to soften your approach a little.

The Huthwaite group who researched the behaviour of successful versus average negotiators found that the successful ones explained their reasons for disagreeing or saying no *before* they voiced the disagreement or dissent. So that for example, rather than saying

'I disagree, I think we should arrange the meeting this week because of the need to establish all the facts as soon as possible'

you should say,

'As we need to establish all the facts as soon as possible, I disagree that the meeting can be postponed until Monday'.

Rather than saying

'No, I don't want you to attend the seminar because I need you to complete the monthly figures'

you should say,

'As I need you to complete the monthly figures, no I don't want you to attend the seminar'.

Build rapport

What exactly is rapport and why is it important?

Rapport is the basis of all good communication. Without rapport you can get things done. With rapport, you can get exactly what you want done, probably in a shorter time and to a better standard. Having rapport means that you have established a certain level of comfort with the person with whom you are interacting; you are 'on the same wavelength', it becomes possible to develop mutual understanding. Liking the other person is not necessary for rapport.

HOW TO BUILD RAPPORT

There are many ways of building rapport, most of them intuitive and unconscious. In most situations and with most people, those intuitive, unconscious ways will work very well and will be all that you need. There are some situations and some people with whom it is harder, but there are some rapport building skills which you can learn to use which will make it possible for you to build rapport with the vast majority of people you come across, whether you like them or not.

MIRRORING

Mirroring means matching certain behaviours of the other person. It sounds both too simple and too dangerous to work well – simple because it seems too easy a technique to make a difference, and dangerous because they might notice you copying them and be offended or annoyed. Used skilfully, it is extremely effective and not noticed by the other person involved.

61

Voice tone and pitch

Matching voice tone, speed and pitch is the easiest way to move towards establishing rapport in a work environment. If you are speaking with someone who has a very different speed, tone or pitch to your own, try moving your own voice patterns closer to the ones they are using and you will find that communication begins to become easier. Look at these contrasting voice patterns and think about how the people using them may jar against each other even before they listen to the content of the message.

Rapid use of words	*with*	Slow deliberate use of words
Loud, aggressive tone	*with*	Quiet, shy tone
High, breathy voice	*with*	Deep voice
Clear precise use of words	*with*	Mumbled or cut off words
Quick sharp delivery	*with*	Slow, drawling delivery
Enthusiastic tone and pace	*with*	Bored, tedious tone and pace

If someone is using a very different speed tone and pitch from you, do not try to change to the way they are speaking exactly, just move your voice in that direction. If you match their voice for a while, you will begin to find that you can lead them to match your voice tone and pitch.

Body posture and movements

Next time you go to a restaurant, look around you at the couples there and spot which of them are in rapport with each other and which are having a fight. The ones who seem to be in rapport will probably have a very similar posture to each other. Not the same, but similar. It is not restricted to couples, the same rule applies to groups. If you look around a meeting that you are in, or a group in earnest discussion of a problem, count how many are sitting in similar ways and be amazed. Look at groups in the canteen, at the coffee machine, or outside the school gate. It is easy to spot those who are not quite as much a part of the group as the others. When you look more closely, you will notice that those in rapport have similar postures and may make similar movements.

Sometimes, old married couples seem to look alike. This isn't true of course, but it may be that their ways of moving, standing, sitting and speaking have become so attuned to each other over the years that they seem to outsiders to look similar to each other.

When you are trying to build rapport by using posture and body movements, you must be careful not to seem as if you are mimicking the other person. Your mirroring has to be subtle and should match in general terms, not match exactly. So for example, if Bill crosses his legs, wait before crossing yours, or cross your feet instead. If Bill puts his head in his hands, move one of your hands to prop up your chin. If Bill suddenly sits up straight as a ramrod, move forward in your chair a little. If he starts thumping the table, put your hands on the table, but don't start thumping!

Before you try simple mirroring in a negotiation, practise in a few situations where it doesn't matter. Try it at a party, on the train, in the pub, making sure it is a no-risk group. Also, make sure that you are in the right mood for strangers to start talking to you! It is easy once you have a little experience and soon becomes something you can do without thinking about it. However, to employ it effectively, you need to feel comfortable and capable when using it.

When to break rapport when negotiating

Establishing and staying in rapport can make your negotiation proceed much more smoothly than it otherwise might have done. If you and your negotiating opposite have been in rapport and sewn up the whole deal, it is sometimes useful to break rapport just before you summarise your agreement and finish, to ensure that even when rapport is broken, you are still comfortable with the deal you have struck.

You can break rapport by standing up, looking deliberately at your watch, giving yourself a shake, or by deliberately changing the speed or pitch of your voice. You can then suggest checking or summarising the actions or concessions which you have both agreed.

SUMMARY

The three elements in putting your case effectively are:

1 Look and sound confident.

2 Be assertive.

3 Build rapport.

1 Look and sound confident by

    (a) dressing to fit the image you want

    (b) lowering the pitch of your voice

    (c) holding up your head and saying words clearly and distinctly.

2 Be assertive by

    (a) being aware of your assertive rights

    (b) knowing what you want

    (c) using an assertive voice

    (d) saying no effectively.

3 Build rapport by

    (a) matching voice tone and pitch

    (b) mirroring body posture.

63

6

Skills and strategies for quick reactions

The skills involved in successful negotiations are those which help you to build a bridge between yourself and the other side, so that you can both meet somewhere in the middle of that bridge. Building the bridge might not always be straightforward. Sometimes in building it, events might not go as smoothly as planned or the first method of construction might not work. Maybe the wrong kind of materials are being used, or there is one key element missing.

In order to be able to build a bridge in the first place, the engineer has to have a certain level of knowledge and skill. Perhaps the first bridge he builds will not be perfect, but as he goes on practising building bridges he becomes more and more skilful and the bridges become better and better.

Negotiating is all about building bridges. In this chapter we look at some of the skills that need to be developed so that the negotiator becomes very good at building bridges and some of the tactics which can help the other person to start to move across the bridge towards her.

Because not all negotiators are in the business of building bridges – in fact, you may come across one or two whose main aim in life seems to be dynamiting not only the bridge but your side of the river as well, we also look at some of the tactics other people might use to achieve their objective.

The main points we consider in this chapter are:

- starting as you mean to go on
- taking time to think
- the use of questions
- making an impact
- strategies used by skilful negotiators
- assessing offers.

Starting as you mean to go on

At the beginning of any negotiation, it's best to know the complete agenda of both parties. One approach to negotiating is to negotiate about one item at a time, only going on to the next item when that one has been satisfactorily concluded. Don't do it. It will not only cripple your bargaining strategy, but antagonise the other negotiator. The requirement is to balance the need to set out the agenda so that both parties know the main goals and desired outcomes of the other side and the need to keep some bargaining counters close to your chest.

To start the process of moving towards each other, both sides need to make some sort of preliminary statement. The best way to start is by asking your opponents what they want to achieve. Sometimes this is seen as a trick so that the questioner will be able to get the better of the answerer. I have seen two groups of people trying so hard to get the other group to state their objectives first that the conversation went something like this.

> 'Would you like to tell us what you want.'
> 'No, we'd like to hear what you have to say first.'
> 'We'd rather find out what you want.'
> 'No, we think you ought to state your position.'

As a start, this was not conducive to good relations during the rest of the negotiation. So start off by asking a question of the other party. but if they are not prepared to answer at this stage, then you start by stating your objective in fairly general terms, i.e. what do you want to achieve.

65

THE FOUR PRELIMINARY STEPS TO A JOINT PROBLEM-SOLVING APPROACH

Step 1: Say what *you* think the two of you are negotiating about.

Summarise what you think you are there for, saying why you think you are meeting, and what you think you want jointly to achieve. This is a crucial point for setting the negotiation off on the right foot, and the sort of approach and language you use here will have an effect far beyond the first few minutes. Use phrases such as:

> 'As I understand it *our* purpose is . . .'
> '. . . discuss what *we* want to achieve . . .'
> '. . . *our* problem . . .'.

Step 2: Ask what *they* think the two of you are negotiating about.

At this stage you are not wanting to hear their detailed proposals for building a three-lane highway at the bottom of your garden, you want to get at their overall outcome – the sort of things they want to reach agreement about. So couch your question in general terms such as:

> 'What do you understand to be our purpose today?'
> 'What are you aiming to achieve from our discussions?'

Step 3: Ask for their opening position.
Do this in such a way that you are still focusing on the problem to be solved rather than on conflicting demands and opposing issues. For example:

'Would you state the problem as you see it'
'Can you outline the position from your point of view?'

Step 4: State your opening position.
Don't be too longwinded about this, but set out your outcome in a direct and factual way. Say what you want to achieve. Make sure that you *look forward to what could happen* rather than back towards what happened in the past. Your aim should be to have both parties focused on looking forward to a positive outcome.

Taking time to think

Thinking on your feet doesn't necessarily mean reacting instantly to every question, statement, fact, proposal, etc made by the other negotiator. Award yourself a little bit of thinking time when you need it. Take the time to picture for yourself what the outcome might be if this suggestion was followed up. Pause if necessary to let your brain get into the right gear for an *appropriate* reaction, not necessarily a fast one.

Obviously, you don't want to have huge silences each time it is your turn to react, nor be so slow off the mark that you don't get a word in edgeways, nor get the reputation of bovine stupidity. Taking your time needn't mean that you react slowly to everything, but that you think before you speak. Sometimes it's easy to have your answer or reply ready and waiting to come out even before the other person has finished speaking. This is especially so if you feel strongly about a particular point and know that you have something worthwhile and important to say. It can also mean that you are not listening properly to the last part of the previous speaker's wisdom – and that if you took time to think, your reaction might be more appropriate and effective. So in order to give yourself valuable thinking time and show that you are in the process of reacting:

- wait until the other person has finished their point before making yours
- if necessary ask for time to think
- make non verbal noises such as 'Hmmm' to show that you are still paying attention and haven't gone into a stupor
- use filling phrases like 'Yes, I see your point there' or 'That's an interesting issue'

■ reflect back on something they have said in your own words, 'So what you are saying is . . .'

The use of questions

Asking the right questions at the right time can be one of, if not the most, powerful tools you have as a skilled negotiator. Questions and the use of them are so important that a whole chapter is devoted to them later in the book.

When someone makes a statement, try to train yourself not to accept it at face value as a fact, nor to react (angrily, defensively, creatively etc) immediately, but to wonder what is behind this statement. Is there a question you could ask? When someone makes a proposal, don't immediately build on it or chop it down. Take some time, ask a question.

When you need some information, ask a question. When someone is angry and emotional, don't escalate the situation by shouting back; ask a question. It's difficult to remain emotionally worked up when you are answering factual questions. Asking questions really is one of the key skills in negotiating, and I recommend that you take the time to read the chapter on how to use them most effectively.

67

Making an impact

When you speak during a negotiation, you want people to listen to you. Listening is one of the hardest things to do well, especially when one's head is full of the next thing to say. So what you say needs to make an impact, it needs to be something which people find easy to listen to.

DRAW THEIR ATTENTION

You may not get people's full attention until you have been speaking for a few seconds; they may be busy with their own thoughts, or just not focused on you, especially in a meeting. So draw their attention by a phrase like: 'I'd like to make a point', 'I'd like to make some proposals', or 'I'd like to set out our position'.

There is one exception to this and that is in situations where you feel inclined to disagree with a statement that has just been made.

Soften disagreement

When you disagree with something someone has said, take the softly-softly approach. Suppose you are having a conversation with a friend and she says that butter is bad for you because it raises your cholesterol level and brings on heart attacks. You disagree with her because you have just read an article which says that people who only ate sunflower margarine had a higher mortality rate than those who ate butter. Which response to your friend is likely to be better received?

'I disagree. I read an article which said . . .', or

'I read an article which said that . . . so I disagree with you there.'

'I disagree' is a very sharp statement. It is an immediate contradiction of what someone has said. There is a good chance that they hear the 'I disagree' and then switch off into some belligerent thoughts of their own, therefore not hearing your very good reasons for disagreeing with them.

GIVE YOUR REASONS

Before saying what you want, briefly give your reasons for wanting it. There is a skill in giving your reasons in enough detail to make your request sound a reasonable one, but not so longwindedly that your audience have switched off by the time you get to the point. Most people have suffered the manager who loves the sound of his own voice so much, or needs to justify his position so repeatedly, that he talks and talks for so long that by the time he has reached the heart of his message, it's too late because everyone has stopped listening. So keep your reasons brief and to the point.

KEEP IT POSITIVE

Make statements about yourself not about them

When you are giving reasons for your requests, needs demands, etc, give those reasons by making statements about yourself, not about them, if humanly possible. If you make statements about your perceptions of the other party, they may be perceived as derogatory, attacking or snide, even if they were not intended to be. So rather than saying 'As you are not able to meet until Friday . . .', say 'As I need to meet you as soon as possible . . .'.

Do not imply blame

If you have to make statements about them, in order to set out the situation accurately, do not use words or phrases which have negative overtones, such as: 'The *problem* arose when you *failed* to complete the work on time', or 'That *unfortunate* omission *on your part* led to Harris and Co getting the contract'.

Instead, try to keep references as neutral as possible, for example: 'When the work was not completed in time . . .', or 'When Harris and Co got the contract . . .'.

Where you have to refer to the past, refer if you can in terms of *we*: '*We* didn't meet the deadline,' or, '*We* failed to come to an agreement about payment the last time we met'.

Strategies used by skilful negotiators

Neil Rackham and his colleagues at the Huthwaite research group, did some research about the skills and methods used by negotiators. They wanted to find out if there were any particular techniques used which made a difference to how successfully negotiations were completed. Their criteria for skilled negotiators were that they should be rated as effective by both sides, they should have a track record of significant success and that they had a low incidence of implementation failure. Note that this is not a difference between good and bad, but average and skilled. So that the skilled negotiators were better than average.

They found that there were a number of techniques and methods used *more* by skilled negotiators than average ones, and a number which were used *less* by skilled than average negotiators. From their work, we can abstract a list of do's and don'ts for improving your negotiating.

69

APPROACHES TO AVOID (DON'TS)

Irritators

Irritators are those phrases which imply negative or derogatory things about the other party, intentionally or unintentionally. If you say, 'We think we are being very reasonable in . . .', you are actually implying that the other party is being unreasonable. We have already come across a fine set of irritators in those sentences which say negative things about the other party such as, 'you failed', 'you did not', 'you insisted'. Irritators are also those words and phrases which apparently have one meaning, but are interpreted as having quite another. For example:

'With respect . . .'	is often interpreted as	'You idiot'
'With deepest respect'	is often interpreted as	'You stupid idiot'
'I hear what you say'	is often interpreted as	'I don't care what you think'

Counter proposals

Sally and Michael are meeting to discuss the best way of organising their firm's contribution to the local charity event – a carnival. Their brief is to combine the best publicity for their firm with raising as much money as possible for the charity concerned. Michael suggests a float followed by a tombola stall. As soon as he pauses to draw breath, Sally suggests hiring a bouncing castle.

How is Michael likely to feel at this point? He will probably feel slighted, overlooked, disregarded. Sally had an idea which she thought was better than Michael's, so she came out and said it. She didn't give any time to considering or at least appearing to consider his idea. So what might happen now? Is it more likely that Michael will consider the pro's and con's of Sally's idea, or go back to his idea and fight for it? Human nature being what it is, there is at least an even chance that Michael will be even more inclined to stick to his idea come hell or high water.

So what should Sally have done? Sally should have asked Michael a few questions about his idea – what sort of float might they have, or what sort of tombola was he thinking about – but not too detailed questions at this stage, she is only asking him to clarify his idea a little. This gives him the chance to say what would be good and useful about the idea. (It also might mean that he would see for himself some of the pitfalls). She could then go on to put her idea forward. 'Another idea might be . . .', or, 'What do you think about . . .?'

70

Defence/attack spirals

Tony from Accounts and Richard from Purchasing are discussing some recent invoices. Tony makes a comment about Purchasing which Richard perceives to be a criticism. It doesn't matter whether or not it was intended as a criticism, it's the perception that is important.

Human beings have the same primitive response to a threat as all other animals. It's called the *Fight or Flight* reaction, and means that the body produces adrenalin to give the energy to run away, or turn and defend itself. As sophisticated animals, this response is not confined to physical threat – verbal attack triggers the same mechanism. Criticism is a form of attack. When Richard is criticised by Tony, he might 'fly', i.e., he might say that yes it was all his fault and he won't do it again. On the other hand, and perhaps more likely, he will 'fight', i.e. he will defend himself.

Defence looks very much like attack. When warriors are defending a besieged city, they tend to throw back at the attackers anything that comes to hand. So when Richard defends Purchasing, he may do so by denying the 'accusation' or by throwing back any small irritant that Purchasing has suffered from Accounts in living memory. In this way, a perceived criticism which is denied, or refuted by reference to someone else's misdemeanour, can escalate into a spiral of attack, defend/attack, defend/attack and so on. How can you avoid getting into a defence/attack spiral?

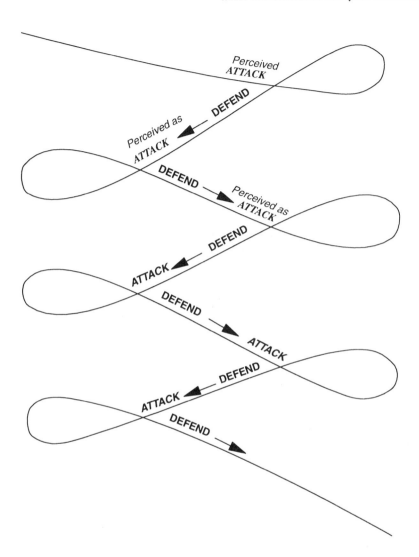

Fig. 6.1 The defend/attack spiral

1 Ask yourself if the criticism is valid or invalid.

2 If the criticism is valid, accept it, but divorce it from the current discussion if possible. 'I accept that we didn't finish on time last time. I'd like to look at how we could make sure that we are both happy with the deadline this time.'

3 If the criticism is invalid, disagree with it calmly, but don't get involved and move on to the situation at hand. 'I don't agree that we never finish on time, but let's look at the deadline we need to meet this time.'

4 If the criticism is partly valid, perhaps exaggerated, agree with any truth in it, disagree with the rest, then carry on with the present business. 'I agree that we didn't finish on time last time. I don't agree that we never finish on time. Let's look at what we have to achieve this time.'

In doing this, you are avoiding an argument while still being able to retain your integrity. Granted, it's easier said than done, but it is a skill well worth practising.

Argument dilution

One of the phrases which is commonly used in the halls of justice is, 'The weight of the evidence'. When we look for evidence to support an idea, or to back up a cause, we tend to think of the weight of the evidence as *how much* evidence we can collect. We look for a number of reasons why the bypass should not be built, or why the school should not be closed, or why we have an inalienable right to three weeks off in August.

Now think of evidence as presented to a court. If a criminal is being charged with a crime, which is more likely to convict him – one really good piece of evidence, such as being caught red-handed outside the bank, or a number of smaller pieces of less clear evidence? One good piece of solid evidence is more effective than a number of lesser pieces. Similarly, one good reason is often more useful than a number of lesser ones. Rackham et al found that skilled negotiators put forward one or two strong arguments for their case, and only if those were unsuccessful, went on to the less powerful arguments. Putting forward all the arguments to begin with tended to lessen the impact of the one or two strong ones.

A couple of years ago, we applied for planning permission to extend our house. We wanted to extend sideways, over the garage, and although many of the other houses in the road had been extended, we were the first ones to want to extend in this direction. Looking from the road, it would have made our house look larger than the others in the road.

One of our neighbours objected to the plans. He was very open about it, and came and told us that he was objecting and why. His main objection was that the proposed extension would make our house look larger than all the others and that if we were given planning permission, many of our neighbours would have the same idea. He thought this would 'alter the character of the road'. Later on he showed us the letter he had written to the planning committee about his objections. The letter ran to three pages of A4 and gave thirteen separate reasons for his objection to our plans. These objections included the fact that the proposed extension would shorten our drive slightly, so we might park our car on the road, and also the possibility that we might not match the colour of the existing bricks. A number of the other reasons matched these examples in triviality.

Our neighbour made the mistake of trivialising his one main, perhaps good, reason by putting in all the other objections he could think of, large, small and very small. The less important objections clouded and obscured the main one so that it too was disregarded by the planning committee.

Three years on, our house is extended, and it fits in very well with the others in the road. Yes it looks slightly bigger from the front, but they are all slightly different anyway. We are still on speaking terms with our neighbour.

RECOMMENDED APPROACHES (DO'S)

The Huthwaite group found that skilled negotiators used some techniques more than average negotiators.

Behaviour labelling

Before making a point, asking a question, proposing a way forward or clarifying, summarising, etc, *Say what you are going to do.* This does three things:

73

(a) it draws attention to you so that everyone at least has the chance to be listening

(b) it allows them to hear the whole of the important part of your message – sometimes it's easy to miss the first few words of things people say

(c) it gives you a chance to formulate your thoughts into a more coherent form, or if you are asking a question, it enables the other person to be mentally prepared.

Some examples are:

'I'd like to make a point. I think that . . .'
'I'd like to make a suggestion. If we were to . . .'
'I'd like to ask a question. What . . .'
'I'd like to clarify something. What was the reason for . . .'
'I'd like to summarise where I think we've got to so far.'

Testing understanding

Skilled negotiators make a point of checking that they have fully understood what is going on. It is an extremely useful technique because it serves a number of purposes

(a) it enables you to check that you have grasped the substance of the conversation

(b) it makes sure that everyone else present also understands

(c) it gives you an opportunity to restate the problem in your own words, which can help you clarify for yourself what it means to you

(d) it acts as a slowing up mechanism, giving everyone a little thinking time.

Use phrases like:

'Can I just check, . . . you are saying that the number three conveyor belt will not be available for another week?'

'Let me just make sure I've understood this fully, . . . your main concern is that the bicycle parts will not be available in that part of Germany.'

'Let me just verify the facts here . . . you want to have time off from 22 December to 9 January and you have enough leave left to cover that.'

Saying what you feel

If you are feeling confused about what is going on, or you suspect that the person you are negotiating with has a hidden agenda, or you think things are beginning to go round and round in circles, then say so – but be careful about how you say it. If you just go on feeling confused, suspecting hidden agendas, getting frustrated, these feelings are likely to disable your thinking from being as penetrating as it could be. So bring the feelings out into the open. There are good and not so good ways of doing this:

(a) *wrong*	'This is very confusing'
(b) *right*	'I feel a bit confused about this'
(a) *wrong*	'I'm sure there's more to it than meets the eye. What are you hiding?'
(b) *right*	'I have a feeling that there's more to this than meets the eye. Is there anything else that's relevant?'
(a) *wrong*	'We're not getting anywhere here'
(b) *right*	'I feel we're getting a bit stuck on this one'

In all the above examples, **(a)** is wrong because you are expressing your feelings in a way that could be taken as an accusation by the other person. They might think you are accusing them of being confusing or hiding something or holding things up. It can be taken as a criticism, and as we've already seen, criticism leads to defence and counter attack. If you use the approach illustrated in the examples **(b)**, then you are saying how you feel about what is going on. It is much less threatening – and no one can argue with how you feel.

Summarising

Summarising is one of the key skills of any interview, meeting, or negotiation. Two sorts of summaries are useful:

1 *Mid-discussion summaries.* Summarising what you believe has been discussed or agreed so far, part of the way through a discussion, is useful because it:
   (a) ensures that everyone agrees with the summary, and gives people the chance to add important points they believe have been omitted
   (b) is a neat way of ending the discussion of one topic and moving on to the next
   (c) can form a bridge between one subject and the next
   (d) provides a succinct recapitulation of points which have been agreed which is often an opportunity for both sides to write them down.

2 *Summarising agreement.* When you arrive at the end of the negotiation meeting, and you have agreed to agree on certain items, or possibly agreed to leave some to be settled another day, or to be referred to another authority, summarise.

When you finish negotiating, you go away knowing what the two of you have agreed, and the other person also goes away knowing what the two of you have agreed. But do you go away knowing the same thing? One of the most frequent mistakes made by inexperienced negotiators is to assume that both parties in the negotiation go away with exactly the same ideas about what has been agreed and is to happen in the future. So, when you come to the end of a negotiation, SUMMARISE,

(a) agree the action which is to be carried out and by whom
(b) agree the items which have not been finalised and need to be referred
(c) agree the time and place of the next meeting if appropriate
(d) agree the timescale of actions
(e) make sure that no action, time or item is left ambivalent.

Assessing offers

Negotiating is about give and take. We have talked a little so far about how to give, how to make offers which are focused on solving the problem. We also need to look at how you assess the offers which are made to you and how you decide whether they could be productive, appropriate or just plain useless?

MATCH OFFERS AGAINST YOUR IDEAL, REALISTIC AND FALLBACK POSITIONS

How well does an offer fit with your prepared Ideal, Realistic and Fallback outcomes? Does it fit within a band which overlaps yours? If it does, how likely is it that the offer is their final one – might you be able to negotiate some movement on it to shift it into a position more favourable to you? If an offer falls within your IRF positions, the situation is fairly simple. You may or may not be able to negotiate slightly more movement, but at least you have the basis for agreement. You will need to assess:

- is this likely to be the best deal you can get at this stage?
- is it really the best offer they are able to make?
- what other potential for movement might there be?
- Is this the best way you can package up the agreement?
- can you strengthen your position and get a better deal by packaging it in a different way?

If the offer does not fall within your IRF positions, the position may be a little more complicated, and more work may need to be done, but all may not be lost.

Is it on the map?

If you think of the negotiation as a map of how to get to a specific destination, could this offer fit on the map at all? Could it be part of an alternative route to that destination? In other words, though the offer may not at this stage fit in to your IRF position, it could be possible that with a little creative thinking or a few modifications, it may lead to a way forward to agreement. Even if it is not immediately useful, it might be possible to modify it into something useful.

Is it final?

When someone makes an offer, they are beginning the process of walking across that bridge towards you. It may be possible to persuade them to move a little further, increasing or improving that offer to make it more acceptable to you. This may mean that you in turn have to do some moving, bargaining concession for concession.

THE FALSE FINAL OFFER

Some negotiators try to force the pace by making 'only' or 'final' offers. Your job is to judge just how final or unique this offer may be. A few questions such as: 'What would happen if we were unable to agree to this offer?' 'How did you arrive at this precise figure?' or 'What would have to happen for you to be able to increase this offer?' can help you in your assessment.

KEEP YOUR OBJECTIVITY

Assessing offers impartially is not always easy. Your objectivity can be affected by:

- the urgency of the matter
- how strongly your values are involved
- your trust or mistrust of the others involved
- the length of time the negotiation has taken.

Some negotiations go on for some time, or are hard fought, or have an apparent imbalance of power between the negotiating parties. On occasions like these, it may seem that any offer is better than none. On other occasions, your strength of feeling about the justice of your case or the motives of the other party can make you suspicious of everything they propose. You can help yourself assess objectively by assessing the **VIP**.

How **V**aluable to you is the offer?
How easy will it be to **I**mplement?
What **P**rice will it cost you?

Value

How important to you is the concession which they are offering? It may be a concession you were looking for or it may be one that you were not expecting. It may be something which doesn't interest you at all. So ask yourself:

'How valuable is this particular point to me?'

'How far does this take me towards my desired outcome?'

'How does it fit in to my ideal, realistic and fallback positions?'

'Could it be a step in the right direction or is it completely irrelevant?'

Implementation

No offer is worth a halfpenny unless it can be implemented. So you need to assess both how genuine and how practical the offer may be. You may need to ask a number of questions about the detail of the offer to be able to assess whether the person making the offer is able and willing to

77

implement it, what the time scale may be, and what restrictive clauses might apply. The real assessment of a negotiation depends on how successfully the agreement is implemented. Checking the viability and authenticity of any offers is an essential part of ensuring implementation.

Price

Very few negotiators are selfless and unworldly enough to make a concession or an offer without wanting and expecting something in exchange. A quick appraisal of value against cost is necessary at this stage. Ask yourself:

'If I accept this, what am I prepared to offer in exchange?'

'How valuable to me is the concession they want in exchange for their offer?'

'Is it a fair exchange?'

'Is it a worthwhile exchange?'

78

Assessing offers in a dispassionate way against objective criteria can help you to make good decisions quickly.

SUMMARY

1 Start as you mean to go on:
- say what you think the two of you are negotiating about
- ask what they think the two of you are negotiating about
- ask for their opening position
- state your opening position

2 Take time to think:
- wait until they finish making their point before making yours
- if necessary ask for time to think
- give non-verbal signals to show that you are paying attention
- use filling phrases
- reflect back

3 Ask questions:
- probe statements
- examine proposals
- seek information
- deflect emotion

4 Make an impact:
- draw their attention
- soften disagreement

- give your reasons
- keep it positive by a) making statements about yourself not them
  b) not implying blame

5 Use the strategies of skilful negotiators:
  - do not use irritators
  - do not make immediate counter proposals
  - do not get drawn into defence/attack spirals
  - do not dilute your argument
  - label your behaviour
  - test your understanding
  - say what you feel
  - summarise regularly
  - summarise agreement

6 Assess offers objectively:
  - match offers against Ideal, Realistic and Fallback Positions
  - check the finality of offers
  - keep objectivity by assessing **V**alue, **I**mplementation and **P**rice

7

Essentials of bargaining

One of the fundamental parts of the problem-solving approach is the willingness to move. Bargaining is where the movement really starts. When the two parties in a negotiation arrive at the bargaining stage, they begin to offer each other various concessions, movements, or compromises in exchange for others. This is a stage at which the ability to think quickly and creatively is an asset.

There are four essential skills involved in effective bargaining:

- giving and receiving signals
- painting a picture of how it could be
- trading
- packaging

Giving and receiving signals

A crucial skill of fast and efficient thinking in negotiations is the ability to both send signals about *your* willingness to shift from your starting position and pick up the signals which the other person is sending about *their* willingness to move. The problem you face is that if either party stands up, starts waving their arms about and shouting, 'I'm prepared to move here', that is an open invitation to the other side to help them to move as far as possible. Although a bridge may be built, the arm waving side may find themselves walking all the way across it into the territory on the other side. So we need to look for something a bit more subtle than that.

You need to be able to send signals that you are prepared to move, while also being able to read signals that the other person is prepared to move. Usually, you will both be sending signals that you might be prepared to move *at a price* – if movement is going to happen it needs to be two way. You might be prepared to move on a particular point in certain circumstances, and those circumstances might also include a significant movement by the other party.

SIGNALLING WITHOUT WORDS

People send signals consciously and unconsciously. The unconscious signals are likely to be through their body language and tone of voice. I don't want to ascribe particular movements to particular meanings here, because body language is much more subtle than that. In fact we are all extremely good at reading other people's body language, even though we might not always be aware of it.

Do you ever sense when people are uncomfortable? Can you often tell whether your work colleagues are in a good mood or not even before they speak? Unconsciously, you will be picking up signals from the people around you every day. You don't just base your opinions, decisions and reactions on the actual words people say. You base them on changes in body posture, facial expression, movement, and tone of voice. In particular, you base them on a combination of these things. In order to be better at picking up and sending signals, bring your awareness of body language into conscious focus. Here are some of the things to look out for.

Tension

Differences in the degree of tension in someone's body. If the person you are dealing with becomes more tense, then it may be because something important to them is being discussed. Tension can show not only in the actual position of the body, but in the overall mobility and tightness of the muscles. Conversely, when people relax, it may be because something has been achieved or possibly because they think they have got their own way, or even because something isn't important to them.

Position

Position of the body. Leaning forward is likely (although nothing in body language is certain) to mean that a person is more involved or interested in that part of the discussion. In combination with different tones of voice and facial expressions, it can also indicate urgency, aggression, or deep commitment.

Tone of voice

This is a type of non-verbal behaviour with which you may already have great skill. It's not what you say, it's the way that you say it. Think of the number of different meanings you can put into 'We really had a great time today'. It could mean you really enjoyed your day. It could also mean that you had a day which had been horrible beyond all expectation. It could mean that today was fine, but you have dire expectations for the rest of the week – and so on.

You can use your skill at using the tone of your voice to give subtle meaning to words when you want to send signals to others. Listen for the message in the inflection and pitch of voice as well as words when you are picking up signals.

Unconscious signals

Remember that in all probability, you will be signalling with your body unconsciously as well. Some of this you can do nothing about and it's best not to worry about it, because the more self-conscious you are about what your body is doing, the less you will be concentrating on what you want to achieve. However, remember that leaning forward with a look of intense concentration on your face just when you get to what you consider to be the most crucial element in the whole package, might just be a bit of a giveaway.

CHECKING FOR CONGRUENCE

Whether you are signalling yourself or observing the signals of others, check the congruence between the verbal message and the non-verbal

message. If you sense that someone is sending messages which are not compatible, check it out by saying something like:

'You don't seem quite sure about that last point. . .',

'I'm not sure that I've understood you correctly. . .',

'You say that . . . but I wonder if there's a bit more to it than that?'

Be aware that everyone has some skill at discerning whether or not someone means what they say, so ensure that you keep your own verbal and non-verbal signals congruent.

SIGNALLING WITH WORDS

It's sometimes easy to miss the signals people send verbally unless you are actually listening for them. Use and look out for phrases such as:

'*At the moment* we can't give you a discount'

'It's not possible *under these circumstances*'

'It *might be possible* to change the size of the sausages *if* . . .'

'*As things stand* we are unable to alter delivery schedules'

'*We might be able to consider* your wishes favourably *if* . . .

Practise using signals yourself, indicating your willingness to move, but not giving away all your bargaining counters at once.

Painting a picture of how it could be

In building your bridge, it will help your opponent start walking across it if you can give them some idea of what life might be like on the other side. Giving your opponent a picture of what life might be like if certain things were to happen can help to move the negotiation along. At this stage, use phrases which do not commit you or them to a specific course of action, but set out some routes you could take to reach your objective.

Suppose we . . . (or suppose you . . .)

This is a phrase which is more tentative than if –, – then, (which we come to later) because it is not actually suggesting a trade, but offering suggestions of how movement could be made. It can be used to suggest movement from both sides. It can be used to push the other side into making a contribution to the moving process, as in example **(a)** below. It is setting the scene for a possible solution or part of one, by painting a picture of what might happen.

'Suppose we were to agree to deliver by the end of the month . . .
- **(a)** how would that change things?' *or*
- **(b)** would you be able to meet your deadline?' *or*
- **(c)** how would that affect your order?'

'Suppose you were to do the job in Norwich next week . . .
- **(a)** and we were to give you some time off in lieu?' *or*
- **(b)** we might be able to give the Acton work to John?' *or*
- **(c)** what would you need, to be able to keep your other work going?'

How would it be if . . .

This phrase is used in a very similar way to, 'Suppose we . . .'. Again, it paints a picture of what the future could be like if a specific course of action is followed. It is non-threatening and tentative. No offers are being made yet, but the possibility of the offer does exist. The difference is that, 'How would it be . . .?' is more of a question for the other side to consider. It is asking them to think about what life would be like if they were to follow a proposed course of action. It is best used to suggest movement on your part, or movement towards each other.

'How would it be if . . .
- **(a)** I agreed to extend the deadline by a week? *or*
- **(b)** you went to Norwich next week and John took over your Action work?' *or*
- **(c)** you reduced your price and we were able to increase our order substantially?'

83

Trading

When you have signalled your willingness to move and painted a picture of what could happen, the next stage is trading one item for another. Movement on the part of both parties usually indicates some sort of trading. If a WIN–WIN outcome is going to emerge, negotiating has to be a process of give and take. Just giving or just taking is the road to WIN–LOSE. There are some rules which can help you to decide instantly if you are actually trading or just caving in.

RULES OF TRADING

1 Give away things which are of little value to you.
2 Try to gain things which you value in exchange for what you give.
3 Only give away things you can afford to give.
4 Make sure that you won't regret it later.
5 DON'T GIVE AWAY ANYTHING WITHOUT GETTING SOMETHING IN RETURN. This may not necessarily be a concrete asset, it may be as intangible as good will, or a peaceful atmosphere at work. It should though be something that you want.

When children at school swap things, they offer one thing in exchange for another. The sophistication of the swap will vary with the age of the child, in years or experience, but usually, even from a very young age, they swap things which they consider to be of equal value. Sometimes when they come home and tell their parents that they have swopped a bar of chocolate for two conkers, the parent will feel that this is not a fair swap. In the case of chocolate for conkers, it is usually too late for the parent to redress the balance as one half of the swap will have been consumed long since, but where three video games have been swapped for an old football, it is not uncommon for parents to reverse the swap and redress the balance as they see it.

Take two seven-year-old boys called Henry and Mark. Henry has brought an old football to school and is kicking it against the wall. A number of other boys are doing the same thing. Mark doesn't have his football at school, but he does have, against all rules and regulations, three Game Boy games in his satchel. Mark wants to play with a football, so he offers to swap Henry the games for the football. To the seven-year-old, at this moment, the football is more valuable than the games. If Henry has had his fill of kicking footballs, he will quite likely agree to the swap. As far as they are concerned they are both getting a good deal. Mark is getting a good deal because the Game Boy games are useless to him at school as he cannot play with them. Henry is getting a good deal because he doesn't want to play with his football any longer and he's always wanted some

Game Boy games. Because they are seven years old, Mark doesn't think about not having any games to play in the evening, and Henry doesn't worry about the fact that he hasn't got a Game Boy. A classic case for a parental phone call!

If you strip away the fact that this was a very unequal swap, which one of them if not both, would probably have regretted later, Henry and Mark had actually got down to some of the basics of good negotiation. They were observing the first two rules, *they were giving away something which was of little value to them, in exchange for something which was of great value.* However, it wasn't a good swap because rules three and four were broken – they were not aware that in fact Mark was giving away something he could not afford to give, and they might both have regretted the deal later.

THE TRADER'S PHRASE BOOK

When you get to the part of the negotiation where you get down to exchanging one concession for another, to offering a movement here in exchange for a movement there, some words and phrases earn their place on the scroll of honour.

If –, – then

This is perhaps the most useful phrase of all.

> '*If* you will agree to working until six tonight, *then* you can have two hours off in the morning.'

> '*If* I agree to this *then* will you agree to that?'

> '*If* you take three pence off each case, *then* I will agree to purchase twice as many.'

> '*If* you are prepared to reduce the price, *then* I might be able to increase the order.'

> '*If* you are unable to make any movement on delivery dates, *then* there are some serious difficulties in the way of resolving this problem.'

If –, – then is a signal of your willingness to move. At the beginning of the trading session, the ifs and thens are likely to be stated in more general terms, as in, 'If you are prepared to reduce the price, then I might be able to increase the order.' Later on, ifs and thens will become more specific, as in 'If you take three pence off each case then I will purchase twice as many.'

Hmm – and

Hmm – and is a positive and effective alternative to *yes – but*. Most people will have been in a situation, ranging from where to hold the office party to what their mother should wear to the event of the year, where they have made many useful and creative suggestions, to have them all met with the loathsome phrase *yes – but*. When you agree with part of the other person's view or want to point out something else which needs to be taken into account, think how you can use *hmm – and* rather than *yes – but*.

'The project needs to be completed by the last week in September.'

'*Hmm – and* we need to take into account the fact that we won't have half the information we require until the last week in September.'

'Our department has twice the number of people than yours, so we need to have a larger share of the floor space when we move.'

'*Hmm – and* we also need to consider that our department needs to have a number of interview rooms available and also requires to store many bulky items.'

Packaging

ALL TOGETHER OR ONE AT A TIME?

I am sometimes asked by groups learning negotiating skills whether it is better to get all your demands out in the open to begin with, or start off with one and when that has been negotiated, to go on to the rest. The story of Caroline, Fenella and the demanding tenant illustrates one answer to that question.

Caroline had a house which she wanted to rent out. She went to an agent, Fenella. It took a little longer than she expected to find a tenant, but eventually Fenella found a young man, who was very anxious to move in as soon as possible. The only problem was that he really wanted a shower and the bathroom in the house had only a bath. He offered to pay three months rent up front if Caroline would put in a shower.

Caroline's problem was that though the bathroom was newly decorated, it did not have tiling, and as the water pressure was such that it wasn't strong enough to put in a shower head on the bath taps, she would have to have an electric shower put in. She decided to do this in the interests of getting a definite tenant who was very keen on the property, as Fenella said she didn't have anyone else suitable.

The drive of Caroline's house had a high lip on it nearest the road. The next phone call she had from the agent said that the young man wanted the lip on the front of the drive lowered so that he could get his car into it. Caroline had a little work done on this, but then discovered that the young man had a very low-slung sports car, so low-slung in fact that it would mean entirely re-laying the drive to meet his needs. At this point she began to feel she was being taken for a ride, and that the agent, who should have been representing her interests equally, was in fact only meeting the needs of the potential tenant.

Caroline began to realise that the bargain of three months rent in advance in exchange for a shower had not in fact benefited her in any way. She did not have a cash flow problem – she had the money for the shower, but had not particularly wanted to spend it. This new demand made her think that she would be better off looking for a different tenant who would be happy with the house as it was.

Her reaction to the request for the drive to be lowered was to say to Fenella that she was happy for the young man to lower the drive at his own expense as long as he met any other costs which might be incurred through doing so – for example if the works were to disturb any water or gas pipes.

What were the tenant's tactics in this case? He was asking for an additional facility (the shower) and offering to pay three months rent up front. So far so good. He was making an offer which he perceived to be a fair one in exchange for what he wanted. The mistake he made was in waiting until after this request had been met before asking for *another* additional facility. He may have done so as a deliberate tactic, or because he had only just thought of the problem. Whatever his motive, the effect was to enrage Caroline, who began to feel that he was trying to screw one concession after another out of her.

Caroline's tactics weren't so hot either. She had complied with the first request without really considering what options she had. Her outcome was to obtain a tenant quickly. She didn't stop to think about the choices she had in the route she took to that outcome. One way was to meet the tenant's request, another may have been to give the tenant permission to put in a shower, or offer to pay half the cost of doing so. She could even have chosen to look for another house agent whom she might have felt had her interests more closely at heart. Having met the first request, the tenant might have thought of her as something of a pushover and been encouraged to add more and more demands to his conditions of tenancy. If Caroline had not stuck firm when she did, the demands might have gone on and on.

As we see in the above example, one reason for presenting your outcomes as a package is that when they are presented and negotiated as separate items, they can have the effect of irritating or even enraging the other party. People like to think that they have negotiated and reached an agreement. When it appears that there are yet more items which have to be agreed, when they thought that agreement had already been reached, the reaction is not usually a favourable one.

PACKAGING PROPOSALS

The advantage with packaging the issues you need to resolve into one problem to be negotiated are:

- It gives you the flexibility of being able to give way on one thing while gaining something else. You don't have to come to a compromise agreement about every single aspect of the negotiation. Perhaps the number of deliveries per day are immaterial to you but very important to the other party. If you can give them whatever they ask on one issue, you may be able to get a better deal on an issue which is more vital to you.

- It means that you can assess the outcome as a whole, to evaluate the concessions they may be offering against the demands they may be making.

- If all the issues to be negotiated are brought out into the open at the beginning of the meeting, problem solving is made easier and potential sources of irritation reduced.

SUMMARY AND CHECKLIST

The four essential skills of bargaining are:
- giving and receiving signals
- painting a picture of how it could be
- trading
- packaging

Polish up your skills in these areas by:

1 Giving and receiving signals
   (a) be aware of the non-verbal signals people send with their body tension and position and the tone of their voice
   (b) ensure that the signals you send with your body and voice are congruent with the actual words you speak
   (c) use phrases which signal your willingness to move without actually committing yourself to doing so, e.g., at the moment, under the circumstances, as things stand.

2 Painting a picture of how it could be
   (a) suggest some routes you might take to achieve your objective by using phrases such as, suppose we . . . and how would it be if . . .

3 Trading. Stick to the rules of trading
   (a) give away concessions which are of little value to you
   (b) try to gain concessions which you value in exchange for what you give
   (c) only give away things you can afford to give

(d) make sure that you won't regret it later

(e) *don't give away anything without getting something in return*

(f) use the trader's phrase book: *If . . . then, Hmm – and*

(g) don't use the loathsome *yes – but.*

4 Packaging

(a) ensure that all needs are included in the bargaining, don't save something as a nasty surprise for later

(b) gain flexibility by being able to give way on one issue while gaining on another

(c) evaluate the situation as a whole problem to solve, not many small isolated issues.

8

Tactics, tricks and threats

Tactic: a procedure calculated to gain some end
Oxford English Dictionary

The use of tactics is implicit in any game or competition. A runner will pace himself for a while before making his final sprint; chess players move certain pieces before others. Because negotiation is often thought of in terms of a game or competition, the notion of tactics is one which often accompanies the subject. If you take the problem-solving approach to negotiating, you will have less need to use tactics in order to achieve what you want. However, there are some tactics which are worth using to help the negotiation move forward to a positive conclusion.

For some people, the mention of tactics implies an element of trickery, of less than straightforward play. Because of this, they feel uncomfortable with the notion. A tactic is really just a way of getting to the place you want and getting the other person there with you. They come in many shapes and forms. It is true that some of them are more ethical and some more effective than others. Some of the tactics used in negotiations do have an element of trickery about them. They will be mentioned here in order to help you to identify and deal with them if someone else tries to use them on you. Threats are a specific form of tactic, which will be dealt with separately.

Whatever your tactics, the important thing to remember is that you will probably have to work or live with these people in the future. People have long memories, especially for occasions where they think they have been treated badly or unfairly, and the notion of an eye for an eye lingers on in the unconscious, even if not in the conscious mind. Put more basically, if you play a dirty trick in order to get what you want this time, watch out for what's coming to you next time you deal with that individual.

Tactics

ADJOURNMENTS

Adjournments are perhaps the only tactic which it is possible unconditionally to label useful and helpful. You may not always need an adjournment as part of your negotiation, but when you are negotiating, do bear in mind that you *can* adjourn. Adjournments are used or even pre-set in some formal negotiations but are severely under-used in most day-to-day negotiations.

What are they?

An adjournment is a break in negotiations, agreed between both parties. It can last for a long or a short period. Often, we think of adjournments as belonging only to formal negotiations such as union–management meetings, but they can also be useful and appropriate even on the most informal occasions.

91

When to use them

If you are negotiating as part of a team it is probable that you will need to adjourn at least once during the course of the negotiating meeting in order to consider the various offers and counter offers which have been made. If you have come to a tentative or suggested agreement, you will probably need to discuss how well it fits with the outcome you had agreed before starting.

If you are negotiating on your own, and you need a little thinking time, ask for a short break for a coffee etc, while you think about what has been suggested so far. Thinking on your feet is partly about thinking quickly as you go along, but also being prepared to state your need for a little thinking time, to allow you to check the quality of your speed thinking.

How to use them

- state your need for an adjournment and the reason for it. You don't have to have any better reason than wanting some breathing space or a cup of tea
- suggest and agree the duration of it
- re-open the negotiation with a summary of where you left off
- avoid bringing fresh issues into the meeting straight after the

adjournment. If it is unavoidable to do so, leave it until you have got back into the swing of the negotiation.

What to use them for

Use adjournments to:

- check that you have covered all that you need to cover
- assess the offers which have been made against your needs
- assess the offers which you have made – are you getting a fair deal?
- use the opportunity to bring the extra information you now have into your wider picture of how you might achieve your outcome. Does this information give you any other routes to follow?
- cool down or allow the other negotiator to cool down
- surreptitiously contact a boss/colleague/friend to ask advice.

DEADLINES

92

It can be a helpful tactic to set a deadline for completing the negotiation. This should not be a time or date cast in stone, but having a deadline means that issues are more likely to be resolved.

PRE-NEGOTIATION POSTURING

Everyone is familiar with the statements made to the media by various unions and management representatives about what might or might not happen if the negotiations they are about to commence do not produce an acceptable agreement.

The GATT trade talks are an example of negotiations which seemed to go on for ever. The rounds often seemed to break off without agreement having been reached. At one stage, agreement in one area was reached only after the United States of America threatened to impose sanctions unilaterally unless agreement could be reached. At another stage the French stated that they were unhappy with the Blair House agreement on agriculture, and proved it by showing the world television pictures of farmers blockading the roads to Paris with dung and burning tyres. All this was done publicly, outside the actual negotiating arena. This sort of pre-negotiation posturing is not confined to the negotiations which make the headlines. The word can be passed around the office that Kate wants those three weeks in August, and that if she doesn't get them, she will make life miserable for everyone else as only she knows how!

It can be useful, on occasion, to have your desired outcome being fairly common knowledge. If the person or group with whom you are to negotiate is well aware of your needs, it can give them an opportunity to think about how they can best negotiate to help you meet those needs. For example, if you are going to tell your boss that you want to do an MBA and that you want to negotiate doing it part-time, at work, having some paid time off and doing some project work, it is a good idea if your boss has some idea of what you are going to be asking and suggesting before the meeting. On the other hand, if you are the intended victim of the 'if Kate doesn't get the holiday she wants' approach, you need to be aware of the implicit threat and deal with it accordingly.

You can choose between two approaches with this type of pre-negotiation posturing.

(a) Pretend that you don't know anything about it and conduct the negotiation in the same problem-solving style that you would have used in any case.

(b) Confront the pre-negotiation posturing in a direct, assertive, non-threatening way by saying something like: 'I've heard lots of rumours about how badly you want a particular holiday period. Shall we start from the beginning and look at all the aspects we need to take into account. Can you tell me what exactly it is you want.'

93

BLUFFING

The false bottom

One tactic which is used by a number of negotiators is saying that they have reached the bottom of the pot when in fact they haven't. It is a tactic which only works well when you are fairly sure that you have reached a fair price and that the other person is on the point of giving in.

When my children were aged seven and five, we spent a few months in Pakistan. One of the less frightening means of transport in Karachi was a horse-drawn carriage. A number of these would congregate outside an hotel near to the place we lived. Having found out a rough guide to the appropriate prices to pay for transport in these vehicles, I approached them, knowing I would have to bargain. The first time was a disaster. Having failed to agree a reasonable price, I turned, meaning to *ostensibly* walk away in the knowledge that the price I had offered was the going rate, and would be accepted if I looked as if I would go elsewhere. Unfortunately, I had omitted to educate the children in the conventions of Karachi bargaining, and having been promised a ride in a horse and cart, they set up a great wailing when it looked as if it wasn't going to happen. On that occasion I paid more than the going rate. That evening, I taught them about bluffing.

The important thing to remember when you bluff, is that you have to be prepared to carry it through, or have your bluff called. If you are going to bluff successfully, you need to have a clear idea of what you will do if it doesn't come off. Suppose the horse-drawn carriage man doesn't accept your fare, are you prepared to find another means of transport?

Asking for more than you want

There is some folklore surrounding negotiating which says that if you want £10,000 you should ask for £20,000. Similarly we are taught that in the bazaars of the East, the starting price asked for an article will be at least double if not treble its value. This is a different sort of bluffing and sometimes it can work against you as people may take you at face value and refuse to negotiate on the grounds that it is entirely outside their capabilities to meet your needs.

In the days when house prices were relatively stable and not subject to huge rises and falls, a colleague saw a house that she liked which was slightly outside her price range. She made an offer for it, not expecting it to be accepted, so was not too surprised or dejected when it was rejected. The estate agent said that the owners could not possibly afford to take less than the asking price. My colleague had seen another house in the area, which she could afford, so made an offer on that. The next day, the estate agent rang and asked her if she had reconsidered her offer. She told them that she really couldn't afford to pay more than she had originally offered and mentioned that she had put in an offer on another house. Immediately, the estate agent agreed to sell her the house she wanted at the price she had originally offered.

Calling a bluff

It is not always easy to tell when the person you are negotiating with is bluffing. You can use the following criteria to help you make an assessment:

(a) How far away from your estimate of their position, is this offer or threat?

(b) What is their past record like – how many final bids or unrepeatable offers do they usually make?

(c) How congruent are their verbal and non-verbal messages?

You take a risk when you decide to call someone's bluff, but that risk has to be balanced against what you might lose if you give in to a bigger demand or accept a lower offer than you would have liked. There may be many aspects of the situation you need to assess, but a few of them could be:

■ how much do I lose by agreeing to this position?

- how much might I gain by challenging their bluff?
- how much might I lose if I challenge the bluff?
- how confident do I feel that this is a bluff and I can get a better deal?
- how much credibility might I lose if I give in too soon?

USE OF EMOTION

Generally speaking, you should try to avoid becoming emotionally involved when you are negotiating. When your emotions are mixed up in what you are trying to achieve, it is difficult to be detached, logical, open to suggestions and change. However, there are occasions when a sincere heartfelt plea can move people into considering actions they might otherwise not have considered, perhaps because they hadn't realised how strongly feelings or values were involved.

Assess impartially any emotionally charged pleas from those with whom you are negotiating. Focus on the problem not on the people, on how you can best achieve an outcome which is equitable and satisfactory to all parties.

95

THE TOUGH STANCE

Some people pride themselves on being 'tough' negotiators. The tough negotiator often thinks that by making high demands in a forceful way he or she will bulldoze their way through the less experienced or less forceful negotiator. They believe that the tougher they are, the more successful they will be. Unfortunately they are often right in that bulldozing is experienced as bullying, and those who are surprised or intimidated by this tactic, do often let them get away with it. The bully often forgets one of those first precepts of negotiating: 'You have to live or work with them again', and the bullied one may well call up reinforcements next time.

People who regard themselves as tough negotiators have high expectations. If you concede things more easily than they do, they may begin to see you as a soft option and push you even harder to get what they want. Remember that you at least are not fighting a war here, or even a battle. Your aim is to solve the problem and you would like if at all possible to get them involved in solving the problem too. But if they are saying, 'No, we absolutely cannot move on this one unless we have huge concessions from your side', do not be tempted to start finding more concessions. Face it out, or you may end up feeling like a loser because you have been doing most of the giving and very little of the taking.

A tough negotiator will probably use body language to show how tough he is. This is an ideal opportunity to use your new skill of matching body language. If he is adopting an upright, energetic style, match it. If he is taking a laid back, you can't afford not to do business with me, type of stance, match that. It will non-verbally give the signal that you are coming from the same place and might be prepared to use the same tricks.

Tricks

Tricks are some of the not so nice tactics other people might use. It is worth having a look at them and how to deal with them.

PLACE

One tactic with which most people are familiar, either by experience or hearsay is the host placing the guest in an unfavourable position, maybe facing into the light, or in a cramped space. The idea is to make the other person feel uncomfortable in some way, perhaps so that they will feel at a disadvantage, or to diminish their power.

Jim and his colleague were the representatives of a staff association. Whenever they met with the Management side for discussions, it was always in the office of the Managing Director. He had a large office, with a vast desk and imposing swivel chair. The visitor's chair on the other side of the desk was similar. In the corner of the room was a small sitting area with low chairs around a coffee table.

Each time they met, Jim and his colleague were met affably, and asked to sit in the comfortable low chairs. The MD would then pull his desk chair around the desk, so as to be facing them, and his colleague would sit in the visitor's desk chair. This was done with the implication of, 'You have the comfortable chairs', but the effect was that Jim and his colleague were always looking upwards towards the MD and his colleague. Jim was very well aware that the effect of this was to make him feel smaller and less powerful than the MD, but he wasn't quite sure what he could do about it. He felt that he was being put at a disadvantage, but that to mention it would be uncomfortable. He wasn't quite sure whether this was a deliberate tactic or being done unwittingly.

What Jim should have done was to say in a straightforward, pleasant non-threatening way, that he felt uncomfortable having to look upwards when having a discussion and ask if they could all sit at the same level. Bringing someone else's tactics out into the open will usually mean that they stop using them. Once you show that you have recognised the tactic for what it is, it becomes useless to the other side. If the difference in seating levels was entirely unconscious, then it would give some useful feedback which might help the MD have more effective meetings with all sorts of other people in the future.

TIME

> 'Ah, Janet, I'm pleased to bump into you. Could you just spare a minute to discuss the amount of wear on those bearings/ who is going to organise the conference/ how we are going to make those cuts in the production budget/ etc...'

Some encounters like this are innocent, equal and useful. But the wily and unscrupulous or just plain thoughtless negotiator can use this tactic to ensure that he or she is better prepared than you are. When you are caught on the hop, you may not have thought enough about what you want, what you can give away, what your ideal, realistic and fallback positions are, etc.

If you know you are not prepared enough for a discussion or negotiation, say so. Suggest another time when the two of you could meet to conduct the business. If it is a fairly trivial matter, you might only need to give yourself a small amount of time, such as going back to your desk to pick up some papers, or go to the coffee machine. If it is a more complex or important issue, arranging a specific meeting to discuss it will be more appropriate than a chance encounter.

97

THE LACK OF AUTHORITY TRICK

You have come to the point where you have almost reached agreement and the other person says that they have the authority to agree to a certain level, but they do not have authority to go beyond that. The level for which they have authority is almost certainly below that which you want to agree. This tactic is used by some negotiators when they feel themselves being moved towards conceding more than they want to. Do you agree a lower level?

Check authority credentials

Real or invented lack of authority can be a problem. If you suspect that it may be a real issue, or a tactic which may be used when the other person is in a corner, it is a good idea to check their authority credentials before starting the negotiation.

Threats

Using a threat is probably the most effective way of escalating a negotiation into a dispute and pushing a dispute into a deadlock. Threats are used much too often in the negotiations we hear about. When news of a potential industrial dispute hits the headlines, it's usually because one side or the other has made a threat. For example:

'If they don't increase our pay we will strike.'
'If they don't do what we want we will apply sanctions.'
'If they don't reinstate those two men, we will strike on Thursday.'
'If they don't accept lower pay we will sack them all.'

Threats are an expression of power but they are also an expression of powerlessness. In effect, the threatener is saying, 'I don't know of any other way to make you do what I want except by threatening you'.

Think back to when you were a child and disobeying your parents. They might threaten you that unless you tidy your room, you won't be allowed to buy sweets. The threat is an expression of their power in that they have the power to prevent you from buying sweets, but it is also an expression of powerlessness, in that all other ways of persuading you to tidy your room have failed.

Some people of course use threats as their first and only means of persuading people to do something. It implies that they have not put enough time into thinking about other ways of achieving their end. The opportunity here for you as a problem-solving negotiator, is not to respond to the threat, but to help them look at the problem and other ways of solving it. The golden rule when on the receiving end of a threat is:

Don't give in to threats, blatant or implied, unless you are left with no other alternative.

Sometimes threats need to be used as a last resort when all else has failed. You will be more effective in your use of threats if you do only use them as a last resort and not as a standard way of communicating. Threats carry more punch and more meaning if they are used sparsely. The tale of the boy who cried 'Wolf!' is familiar to everyone. If you threaten every day no one will believe you, but if you threaten once a year, people will be more inclined to take the threat seriously.

Threats come in many shapes and forms, some overt and blatant, some more subtle or indirect. If you use threats as a tactic, they should be handled with care, as they can backfire when least expected. They can be a difficult tactic to recognise, as they are sometimes hidden under a veneer of helplessness or even cooperation. Threats are common in international and industrial disputes. They are used for a number of reasons.

- as a reminder of the power balance
- as an attempt to intimidate
- as a show of disrespect or disregard for the other party.

The effectiveness of threats depends on

(a) the credibility of the threatener's intention to carry out the threat
(b) the capability of the implemented threat to damage the other person.

TYPES OF THREAT

Threats come in different shapes and forms.

Compliance threats warn about what will happen if you don't comply with a request, suggestion or ultimation:

> 'If you don't do your homework, you won't be allowed to watch the television.'

> 'If you don't finish the building work by 1 May, you will have to pay a penalty.'

> 'If you don't improve your work, we will have to start disciplinary procedures.'

Deterrence threats warn that if you do carry out a certain course of action, something unpleasant will happen to you.

> 'If you park your car here, it will be clamped.'

> 'If you persist in coming in late, you will have to see the Supervisor.'

> 'If you break the law you will be punished.'

A good example of the difference between compliance and deterrence threats is that of the hijacker. The hijacker will use a compliance threat to try to extort money. 'If you release some terrorist suspects, then I will release the people on the plane.' Whereas the deterrence threat would be a law passed which said that hijacking a plane would carry a mandatory life sentence.

99

THINGS TO REMEMBER ABOUT THREATS

Implementing a threat might impose costs on the threatener

If a buyer threatens not to buy unless the price is reduced, they run the risk of having to spend a lot of time and trouble trying to find another supplier of the same quality and price, in order to implement that threat.

Threats have to be credible

If a manager habitually threatens staff with the sack for minor mis-demeanours such as occasional lateness or one badly presented piece of work, she is unlikely to be taken seriously by any other than the newest and most gullible of employees.

Threats have to be carried out if they are to be believed next time.

A teacher who threatened to keep the whole class in for an hour after school every day for a week and did not carry out the threat because it would have been much too hard to implement without a lot of explanation to parents, quickly lost credibility with his class.

Sometimes threats have the effect of making the threatened more belligerent, and more likely to issue counter threats

Remember the playground? 'I'll tell my Dad', answered by 'My Dad's bigger than your Dad'.

The same *kind* of exchange happens daily in international negotiations. 'My country will impose trade sanctions on your country', countered with 'Well my country will impose trade sanctions on you – but worse'.

The language I have used is perhaps a little simplistic, but the gist of the message is accurate.

Threats are an expression of power

Threats are often made to demonstrate that if you do or don't do something, the threatener has the power to cause something nasty to happen to you. One question you might ask yourself though: if they are so powerful, why are they negotiating with you? Why not just go ahead and do the thing they want to do anyway? Usually the answer will be that although they have power in one arena, you may have power in another. They probably need to work with you – which of course gives you power too.

Most of the time, if we are vulnerable to a threat, so are the opposition

It's no wonder that threats produce counter threats. A threat is a form of attack, which is often defended by a counter attack. If someone has the capacity to cause something unpleasant to happen to you or your organisation, you probably have the power to cause something different but equally unpleasant to happen to them.

IMPLIED THREATS

These are threats which are never actually stated as a threat. They skulk under the surface, waiting to come out as real threats if the hint isn't taken. 'You'll have to do better than that', implies that if you don't you won't get the business. For example,

> 'Did you know that Walker and Quick are making your sort of widgets now?'
> 'We all tend to work until at least seven o'clock in the evening here.'

'I'm sure you appreciate that there may be difficulties if the report is not well received.'

One of your most devastating counters to any threat, but perhaps most of all to an implied threat is that it doesn't really concern you whether the threat is carried out or not. In the case of overt threats it can be an overt response, the most effective response to an implied threat is an implied disregard of it. 'Yes, I know about Walker and Quick. Of course, our type of widgets have a very wide market.'

UNINTENTIONAL THREATS

Casual remarks can sometimes be taken as a threat and thrown back as a challenge. If you were the originator of 'Did you know that Walker and Quick are making your sort of widgets now?', said as an innocent remark, made out of interest, you might originate an entirely unexpected response. If you unintentionally say something which is interpreted as a threat and produces an angry or defensive reaction, try to avoid the, 'I was only . . .' response. It sounds defensive. However, don't put the blame on them for the wrong interpretation. Apologise for having said something which was easily misinterpreted, then move on to giving the correct message clearly.

101

SUMMARY AND CHECKLIST

Tactics, tricks or threats often feature in negotiations. You may choose to use them very selectively yourself, but you need to be aware of them when used by others.

1 Tactics
   (a) Adjournments are a useful and helpful tactic to use:
   - to check that you have covered everything
   - to assess and compare offers
   - to review information
   - to cool down
   - to ask advice
   - to have a rest
   (b) deadlines encourage everyone to resolve issues without unnecessary delay
   (c) choose whether to ignore, confront or use pre-negotiation posturing
   (d) be prepared to carry through your bluffs, or challenge the bluffs of others
   (e) try to avoid becoming emotionally involved yourself, and dispassionately assess the emotional pleas of others
   (f) do not be bullied or bulldozed by negotiators who take a 'tough' stance. Be prepared to stand your ground if necessary

2 Tricks

   (a) confront people who try to put you at a disadvantage with the place or time they choose to negotiate

   (b) check authority credentials before you start to avoid being caught by the 'lack of authority' trick

3 Threats

   (a) don't give in to threats, blatant or implied unless you are left with no other alternative

   (b) the effectiveness of threats depends on the credibility of the intention to carry it out and the amount of damage it could cause

   (c) implementing a threat can impose a cost on the threatener

   (d) threats need to be carried out if credibility is to be maintained

   (e) threats can cause aggression and inspire counter threats

   (f) threats are an expression of power

   (g) implied threats can be just as powerful as actual threats

9

Listening:
getting the whole picture

Why is listening important in negotiating?

You might as well ask, 'Why do you need to put petrol in the car?'. You cannot *negotiate* without listening. You can demand, bludgeon, coerce and concede, but unless you are prepared to listen to what the other person wants, you cannot negotiate.

But why do we need a whole chapter about listening? For those of us fortunate enough to have hearing, it is something we can do without thinking about it. And therein lies the problem. Because the listening we do without thinking about it is not necessarily effective listening. Effective Listening means not only hearing what someone else has said but understanding and mentally filing it. If you have really listened to what the other person has said, you will be able to process the information they have given you and either discard it as not useful, file it away for further reference or ask a question to find out more about it.

At its best, you understand not just the words, but the meaning, of the person who is speaking. You fully understand the content and the context of what they are saying and the feelings which are represented by the words and non-verbal signals of the speaker. It is almost as if you can 'get into the head' of people operating from a different perspective, holding your own assumptions and beliefs to one side while being open to understand theirs. Good effective listening is an essential part of getting the most out of a negotiation. Without it, you can never be sure that:

- you are fully cognisant of as many of the facts of the case as the other negotiator is prepared to tell you
- you are able to pick up the nuances of the messages which might otherwise be mixed
- you have fully understood the implications of a proposal
- you understand some of the feelings and motives of the other negotiator.

Listening effectively is not easy. When teaching a group of senior managers skills for chairing meetings, I video-recorded the meetings they chaired and replayed edited highlights during the feedback session. More than half of them identified times during the meetings when a participant had made a point which they had not really heard. 'I didn't realise you had said that', was a common reaction. They all identified how difficult it had been to chair the meeting and simultaneously *listen* to what was being said at the meeting.

BAD LISTENING HABITS

One of the reasons why it is so difficult to listen well is that in everyday life we fall into habits of careless listening.

Mental ear plugs

There is a big difference between listening and hearing, though it is difficult to listen well if surrounding noise is loud or distracting. However, surrounding noise has a more important and sinister part to play in an inability or disability to listen effectively. Because we are surrounded by noise most of the time – in increasingly popular open plan offices, in shops with piped music, at home with the background of the radio or television, we learn to tune out sound. *We develop the ability to think our own thoughts, develop our own ideas, without being influenced by the sounds around us.* We develop the ability to put in mental ear plugs, hearing the sounds around us, but not listening to them. We actually learn not to listen.

We also have a tendency to put in the mental ear plugs when we are concentrating on something. Speaking to colleagues when they are absorbed with a problem may have as limited an effect as speaking to your partner when he or she is immersed in a book or a television programme. The person concerned speaks to you and appears to answer the question you may have asked them, but make a further enquiry about the matter later and they may not even recollect speaking to you about it. This learned ability to hear without listening can be a real disability when listening to understand becomes important.

Cursory interpreting

The way we use language leaves huge gaps for the listener to fill in with their own experience and understanding, so listening is about interpreting. When we listen, we interpret what the other person really means by what they say. Everyday conversation teaches us to be lazy listeners because much of the time, it doesn't matter if you don't understand the exact meaning of what someone is saying. The general gist is enough for you to be able to live and work together perfectly adequately.

Superficial listening

People listen superficially, hearing the first part of what the speaker says, then switching off for the rest. When your friend starts describing their holiday in Florida, you will not be giving him your full attention if you are just waiting for him to draw breath to tell him about your sojourn in the Lake District. This is especially true when people believe that they are going to disagree with the person who is speaking. So when Joe opens his mouth and starts talking about the reasons why the union is demanding a 10 per cent rise and three extra days holiday, the management side may be more concerned with waiting to get across their reasons why the rise needs to be 2 per cent tied to productivity than really listening to and understanding Joe's point of view.

BUSY MINDS

When doing a demanding task such as negotiating, chairing a meeting or interviewing, you may believe you are listening, but your mind is also dealing with so many other demands such as what your next point will be, how you will best respond to this, can you give up x to achieve y, or how much you disagree with this man, that you are not taking in the whole of what is being said. When concentration is focused on internal concerns, the brain seems to edit out what the other person is saying.

FAILURE TO LISTEN

Failure to listen effectively is arguably one of the greatest causes of misunderstanding and friction in the world. Considered purely at a domestic level, there will be few homes in which a conversation has not taken place which goes something like this:

> 'You never told me we were . . .'
> 'I *did* tell you – you weren't listening to me.'

At a domestic level, this may lead to a greater or lesser row, depending on the importance of the subject matter and the relative amicability of the relationship of the participants. At a more global level, whether we are talking about working relationships, business deals or international misunderstandings, failure to listen effectively can have devastating effects.

Listening with the whole person

Effective, extended, active listening involves listening with the whole person. Not just using the ears, but the eyes, body, voice and emotions. It means using all your senses to take in and understand not just the words that someone is saying, but the message behind the words.

LEARNING TO LISTEN

Part of learning a skill is becoming aware that it exists and that you need to increase your competence at it. The model of unconscious to conscious competence illustrates this very well.

- **Unconscious incompetence**
  I have never driven a car so I don't know how difficult it is.

- **Conscious incompetence**
  On my first driving lesson I realise how bad I am at driving this terrifying machine.

- **Conscious competence**
  When I take my test, I am a competent driver, but still very aware of what I am doing.

- **Unconscious competence**
  After a number of years driving, I drive carefully but I don't have to think at all about the mechanics of operating the car.

If you have read most of this chapter, you should by now have got to the stage of conscious incompetence. The rest of the chapter is aimed towards helping you move at least to conscious competence, if you are prepared to put in the practice.

ACTIVE LISTENING

It is possible to learn to listen effectively. Effective listening is often called Active Listening. It is a very demanding skill because:

(a) you have to concentrate, giving your full attention to the speaker – to their words, non-verbal signals and tone of voice

(b) you need to be able to respond calmly, with patience and empathy even when someone is expressing ideas which you feel to be misguided, illogical, or generally and totally wrong.

MODELLING

Modelling is one of the most natural and effective ways of learning. All children use modelling as their means of learning behavioural patterns from their parents and peers. When people are taught a mechanical skill, they usually learn it by copying (modelling) someone else who is expert at that skill. When you want to learn a new skill, one of the ways of doing it is to consciously model the behaviour of someone who is already very good at it. What *exactly* is it that they do? What are their patterns of non-verbal behaviour? What are their speech patterns? What are they thinking and feeling in order to achieve the result that they do. Let us try to apply modelling to effective listening.

Think of someone you know who is a good listener. Bring into your mind a clear picture of them the last time they were listening. What were they doing? What was it about their listening that makes you label them a 'good listener'? They probably had some, if not all, of the following characteristics:

- attentive posture, fairly still
- no fidgeting, doodling etc
- looking at the speaker *all the time*
- occasional nodding
- facial movements that fitted the story, i.e. appropriate smiles etc
- an impression that they understood what the speaker was feeling
- appropriate tone of voice
- occasional pertinent questions
- a word here and there to encourage the speaker to continue
- an occasional replay in their own words of what the speaker had said.

107

NON-VERBAL SIGNALS

Non-verbal communication is the most basic and primitive form of communication. We are led to believe that our ancestors communicated in grunts before the advent of language, and the many wildlife programmes on television can leave us in no doubt that animals communicate with each other without the ability or need for speech. When humans find themselves in a country where they are unable to communicate in the local language, non-verbal signalling is an effective way of achieving the basic necessities of life. Many of the non-verbal messages we send day to day are unconscious, and are noted and interpreted unconsciously by those receiving them. One of the most effective ways of increasing your listening skill is to increase your awareness of the non-verbal signals that others are sending. Similarly, the non-verbal signals you make are the clearest way you have of sending the message 'Yes, I'm listening to you'.

There is a big danger with bringing your own non-verbal signalling into consciousness. That is that you will become so concerned with getting the non-verbal signalling correct that your attention is taken from the listener to yourself. So in looking at the non-verbal signals you send, let us concentrate on the easiest to put into practice.

BODY MOVEMENTS

Show your attentiveness by having a certain stillness, a complete lack of fidgeting, squirming or twitching. The only movements will be those which help the listening rather than detract from it. Movements which help listening are a degree of head movement, indicating agreement or signalling to continue, and those which help rapport building by roughly matching the speaker's posture.

Eye contact

Eye contact is one of the ways in which we signal to others that we are listening. This is why it is so infuriating, embarrassing or frustrating to talk to someone who does not look at you. When you speak to a person who carries on writing, looking at the television, searching through the filing cabinet or rummaging in their desk drawer, even though they may say, 'Carry on, I'm listening', you are unlikely to feel that you have their full attention. We have a friend of long standing who turned up one day with a new girlfriend. When they eventually left, we decided that she had not gained the seal of approval. On further analysis, we realised that when we had spoken to her or she had spoken to us, she had not looked at us for any length of time – a fleeting glance had been the longest eye contact any of us had had with her. As we could not consider her shifty, we had interpreted her behaviour as dislike, disapproval or a lack of interest in us.

A listening exercise often used with groups is called 'Sabotage'. One person in a pair is asked to talk to the other. The other is asked to deliberately show that they are not listening in any way that they choose. The 'listeners' often look out of the window, pick their nails, rummage in their handbags etc. The interesting thing about this exercise is that even though the speakers know that they have been set up in this way, they still have feelings of irritation, frustration, or even anger.

When we have a conversation, we have certain unconscious behaviours and expectations about eye contact. There is a speaker's pattern and a listener's pattern. Consciously notice the eye contact you have during your next conversation and you will find it goes something like this. The person who is speaking looks at the listener, most, but not all the time. He may briefly glance down at his papers, look at the ceiling or out of the window for inspiration, then back at the listener again. But when he does look back at the listener, *he expects the listener to be looking at him*. The listener is not expected to look out of the window, but to look at the speaker all the time.

When it is the listener's turn to talk, the speaker will look at him in expectation. The listener now turned speaker will look briefly away, then fall into the speaking pattern of eye contact. Looking constantly at the person to whom you are listening is one of the best ways of focusing your attention on them and starting the active, effective listening progress.

Listening on the wide band means observing the non-verbal signals of others.

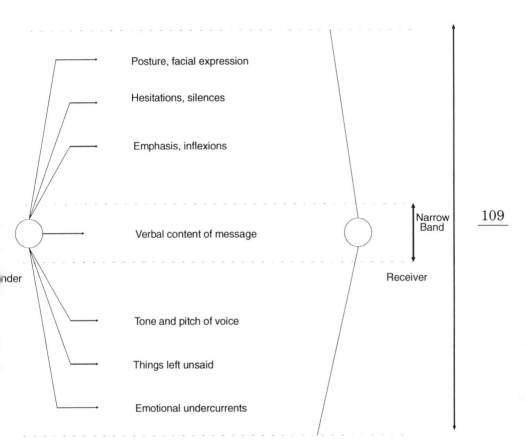

109

Fig. 9.1 Wide band listening

Eye contact plus

Use your eyes to pick up signals from the speaker's non-verbal behaviour. The way they sit, the movements they make, changes in muscle tension, skin tone and breathing pattern are all parts of the unspoken message which accompanies the spoken one. If you pay close attention to the person who is speaking, you may well pick up these messages consciously or unconsciously. Don't worry about interpreting them in isolation, as they are just part of the message – the words and voice making up the whole of it. Actively observing the non-verbal signals of the person to whom you are listening, in this way, is a part of focusing your whole attention on them.

Words apart

Use your ears to be aware of changes in the tone, pitch, speed and continuity of the speaker's voice. The verbal content of the message can be enhanced or changed by hesitations and silences, changes of emphasis or inflection, things that are left unsaid. All these give clues to the meanings and emotions behind the words. Think about how many different meanings it is possible to give to the phrase, 'I'm delighted you came'. It can mean, 'I'm delighted you came; I'm really sorry you came; I'm pleased *you* came, pity about the rest of them coming; *I'm* pleased you came, even if no one else is.' Similarly, when a colleague comes into the room and says, 'I've been chosen to give a presentation about the African project to the Board', you will probably be able to tell from her tone of voice whether she regards this as a thrilling opportunity or her worst nightmare.

Testing understanding and clarifying

Testing understanding can profit you in two ways:

(a) You ensure that you really do have the facts correctly.

(b) You demonstrate that you have understood what the speaker is saying.

Getting the facts correct is one of the fundamentals of active listening. It is essential to ensure that you are receiving the message you think you are. The simplest way of doing this is to rephrase what the speaker has said and repeat it back to check whether or not you have heard and understood accurately. Use phrases such as:

> 'So can I just check, what you are saying is . . .'

> 'As I understand it, you are proposing . . .'

> 'So your point is that . . .'

> 'Let me just be sure I've understood correctly, you need . . .'

Reflecting

Effective listening means understanding the feelings and emotions tied up with the facts as well as the facts themselves, and ensuring that the speaker is aware of your understanding. Reflecting means picking up and interpreting what people say, and then feeding your interpretation back to them. This is where you demonstrate your understanding of the meaning of the words *plus* the non-verbal signals. For example:

'You say that you would like to take on this job, but you don't sound very sure about it.'

'You seem to be very determined that delivery has to be included as part of the package.'

'You mentioned the need to keep the budget under £50k, but I wasn't sure how definite a criteria that was.'

Questioning

Questions have many uses – so many in fact that there is a whole chapter devoted to them – but one of their functions is to demonstrate and enhance listening. Asking questions may seem like an odd way to listen, but asking pertinent and discerning questions which follow on from what people have said and encourage them to develop the subject in the appropriate direction, is a crucial listening skill. It is a particularly important skill in negotiating, after you have picked up what seems to be the main issue, to ask a question which will encourage the speaker to expand his argument or develop his theme. For example:

111

'You mentioned metal fatigue – how important is that?'

'When you say you need to move fast on this problem, how fast are you talking about?'

'What specifically is the problem with the journey?'

Summarising

Summarising is so useful, that it should not be left to the end of the negotiation. It demonstrates your listening and understanding and has three other important benefits:

1 It clarifies and reinforces the message for both speaker and listener.

2 It gives the speaker the opportunity to correct the listener if they summarise incorrectly.

3 It finishes off one subject, creating the opportunity to move on to another.

'So the main problem seems to be that the computer network is not available before 06.00.'

'So we have agreed that you will undertake to do the research on bivalves, while I investigate the need for trial instruments.'

'As I understand the position so far, your proposal is that our company should bear the cost of servicing this equipment. I have suggested that we should bear that cost for the first twelve months and that after that it should be the subject of a separate agreement. In return, . . .'

LISTENING TO HELP YOURSELF

It's all very well listening to what someone else has said, but this is a book about negotiation after all, not counselling. So what about the problem incurred by people like the managers practising chairing meetings in our example at the beginning of the chapter, who are trying to listen while also trying to ensure that they make their own contribution count? Listening needs to be worthwhile, to benefit the listener at least as much as it benefits the speaker. It is worth bearing three facts in mind:

(a) it is very hard indeed to think and listen at the same time

(b) it is sometimes possible to concentrate so hard on listening that you don't actually take in a word of what is said

(c) fully understanding what someone has said means that you have better quality information on which to base your next move.

Negotiating is certainly no easier than chairing meetings. You have a lot to think about, many balls to keep in the air at once. Thinking and listening at the same time is very nearly impossible for most mortals. The ability to listen well must therefore be linked to the ability to think very rapidly after you have listened.

Figure 9.2 illustrates the sort of thing that often goes on as we listen. Listening is surrounded and sometimes engulfed in thinking. That thinking may be about what you want to say next – or it may be to do with, 'Next I have to summarise to show that I have understood what he's said so far'.

Figure 9.3 illustrates a different way of operating. The listening, by focusing the whole attention on the speaker, is not distracted or diluted by thinking. Keep the thinking part of your brain available but separate and switch between them as necessary.

As with all skills, the more you practise, the more proficient you become. The good thing about listening skills is that you don't have to wait until you are in the vital negotiation before you can practise them. You can practise every day on your colleagues, friends, partner and

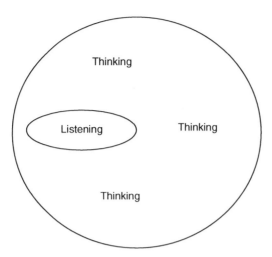

Fig. 9.2 Listening is surrounded and may be engulfed by thinking

113

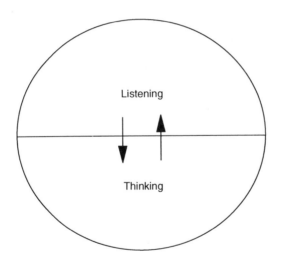

Fig. 9.3 Thinkiing and listening kept separate, with rapid switch available

children. As you practise, notice what was easy or difficult, and make sure that you have an opportunity to practise the difficult parts again soon.

SUMMARY AND CHECKLIST

Listening is one of the core skills of good negotiating and can make a big difference to the quality of information you collect, which in turn can affect the outcome of the negotiation. You can help yourself to listen better by

1 Being aware of and trying to avoid the bad habits of listening which are easy to fall into:
   - hearing without listening
   - poor interpreting of what is heard
   - superficial listening

2 Understanding that when your brain is busy with other demanding tasks, it often lets listening take second place.

   Learn to listen effectively by:

3 Concentrating, giving your full attention to the speaker.
4 Modelling someone whom you believe to be an excellent listener.
5 Using non-verbal signals to indicate that you are listening.
6 Testing your understanding and clarifying what you have heard.
7 Reflecting back feelings and emotions.
8 Asking questions to encourage people to develop a subject in the appropriate direction.
9 Summarising regularly throughout the discussion.
10 Listening on the wide band to help yourself do your job more effectively.

Asking the right questions

I keep six honest serving men
(They taught me all I knew);
Their names are What and Why and When
And How and Where and Who.

Rudyard Kipling

The Elephant's Child, in the Just So stories, knew what he was talking about. Questioning skill is perhaps the most seriously underrated management tool which is relatively easy to learn, to practise and to improve.

Questions are one of the key tools of the effective negotiator. You can use questions to avoid stalemates, diffuse anger, give you thinking time, stimulate creative thinking, find out people's visions and motivations, as well as the usual collecting or clarifying information. The list of useful jobs for questions is endless. Throughout this book, the use of questions has been advocated in many places. In this chapter, we look at the uses of questions in more detail than they appear in the other chapters in the book. These uses go beyond the run-of-the-mill questioning skills you may have learned for selection interviewing or communication skills.

We will look at:

- why questions are a vital part of the negotiating process
- basic questioning techniques
- some less familiar questioning techniques
- creative uses of questions in negotiations including:
  - questions to establish the big picture
  - questions to get out of stalemates
  - questions to clarify details
  - questions to stimulate thinking
  - questions to gain commitment
  - questions to ask for feedback
  - questions to float ideas
- questions to avoid
- using questions conversationally
- questions as a response to conflict

115

Why are questions so vital?

DELETIONS, DISTORTIONS AND GENERALISATIONS – MAKING SENSE OF THE NON-SPECIFIC

The language we use day to day does not always convey *exactly* what we mean. Most of the time it is sufficient to convey the *sense* of the message. Conversation would become very tedious and longwinded if we did try to convey exact and specific messages every time. For example, in late October, you may say to a friend, 'I travelled through Burnham Beeches today and the trees were wonderful'. Your friend, being aware that trees change the colour of their foliage in the autumn, will understand the content and context of what you are saying, based on their own experience of autumn foliage.

In this case it was unnecessary to be specific. But if your friend happened to be a native of a tropical island or an arctic landscape, you might have a little more explaining to do. If that were so, you would need to expand your statement, not just to say that the leaves of the trees change colour in the autumn before dropping off the trees, but being even more specific. How could we describe what happens so that someone *without* the necessary experience understands what we are talking about?

> 'The leaves of the trees change colour gradually, from green to yellow to orange to red to brown. Not all the leaves on the same tree change colour simultaneously, so that on the same tree, the leaves are different colours. Where there are a number of trees together, each tree may be a different colour, especially when there are different varieties of trees as these change colour at different rates. Some varieties of trees change to darker reds and oranges than others . . . etc.'

It is no wonder that we delete content and generalise when we speak to others! In fact, when people give explanations or describe things or recount events, their listeners are unlikely to notice that what they are saying is full of generalisations and deletions. When we speak a message, the words we use represent a much fuller framework. When someone else hears the message, they understand it by relating it to their own framework. The diagram below shows how this works.

Most of the time this method works very well, but it can cause problems if the framework of the person sending the message is significantly different from that of the person receiving the message. When it is important that you are certain of *exactly* what someone means, as in a negotiation, then the parts of the message which are omitted or left to common experience or assumptions may need to be clarified. Questions

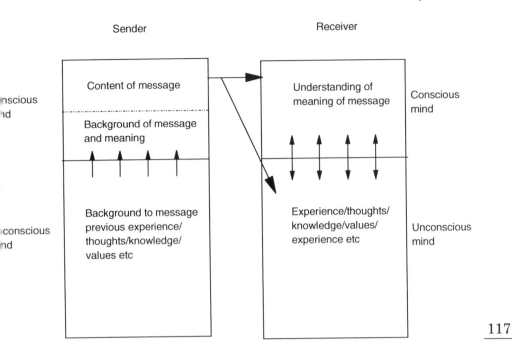

Sender   Receiver

Content of message   Understanding of
                            meaning of message
Conscious   Conscious
mind   mind
Background of message
and meaning

Background to message   Experience/thoughts/
Unconscious   previous experience/   knowledge/values/   Unconscious
mind   thoughts/knowledge/   experience etc   mind
               values etc

117

Fig. 10.1 Sending and receiving messages

are the tool you can use to untangle or dissect what someone means, especially when they have *assumed* that you will understand without explanation.

MIND READING

The mind reading people use day to day is not the mind reading of conjuring tricks, such as, 'Pick a card and I'll tell you what it is', but the everyday occurrence when you *know* what someone was going to say when they had hardly opened their mouth. You can even know (or think that you know) what someone was thinking, when they haven't said anything at all. This sort of mind reading is an intuitive response to a number of non-verbal clues. The most obvious of these is facial expression or tone of voice, but may also include change of skin tone, movement, pace and pitch of the voice. The mind reading may be very accurate, or complete hallucination, or an expression of what we ourselves would think or feel in that situation. We have the capacity to project our own unconscious thoughts and feelings and then experience them as coming from the other person.

In some ways this ability can be very useful, for example, if two people are working together 'on the same wavelength'. It can be a stimulating and productive experience to be able to communicate ideas very quickly because one person is able to interpret the half-finished ideas of the other. In other cases, it can be dangerous, offering huge opportunities for misrepresentations and misinterpretations of what a person is thinking or feeling.

For an example, when great aunt Mabel gives fifteen-year-old Mark a bobble hat for Christmas, it is relatively easy to interpret correctly his reaction to this gift. However, it is all too easy to take this ability to interpret reactions and apply it in inappropriate situations. If you make a proposal during a negotiation and the other person goes silent, you may be thinking to yourself, 'He doesn't like it, he is just sitting there thinking about how he can sabotage this/how he can break it to me gently/of all the reasons why this won't work/etc'. In this case, you may be making a dangerous assumption, which could lead you to start talking about how you could amend or improve your proposal, before the other person has had a chance to give his considered opinion to the first one.

THE ABSTRACT AND THE CONCRETE

Laborde, in *Influencing with Integrity* (1983), distinguishes between 'fat words' and 'lean words'. Fat words are abstract, non-specific words, which can mean many different things to different people, for example words like integrity, productivity, respect, difficulty. Lean words are concrete, specific words, where it is much more likely that everyone will have the same understanding or picture in their mind. Banana is a lean word, as is desk or chair. Yes, there are many varieties of banana, desk and chair, but the prospect of misinterpreting the concepts is very small.

Fat words are useful because being general, the audience can agree with their own interpretation of the word. They are used to gain agreement. Lean words on the other hand are necessary to get tasks done and decisions made. Fat words are useful when agreeing that you have a basis for negotiating, as it is easier to find a shared outcome when it is non-specific. On the other hand, lean words are essential in other parts of the negotiation when you are agreeing on decisions, concessions and outcomes.

When you are negotiating, it may be necessary to translate fat conceptual words into lean factual words, or conversely to change the lean to the fat. Questions are a tool both for finding out the abstract concepts of the other person and for refining and defining those abstract concepts into concrete proposals and decisions.

Basic questioning techniques

Some questions are more efficient at gathering information than others. Many people will be familiar with the distinction between open and closed questions.

OPEN AND CLOSED QUESTIONS

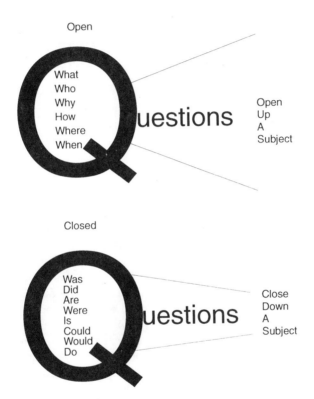

119

Fig. 10.2 Open and closed questions

Open questions open up a subject. They encourage people to answer in whole sentences and begin to tell a story. Closed questions are better at closing down a subject. They encourage people to answer mono-syllabically to confirm or deny the question.

Open questions start with the following words or phrases. Most of them are WH words:

What . . . (does your current supplier offer you?)

Who . . . (else is involved?)

> Why . . . (is this point important to you?)
>
> How . . . (do you do this task at the moment?)
>
> Where . . . (do I need to look for this information?)
>
> When . . . (is the deadline for this decision?)

And one which would not have scanned in Kipling's poem (and is not strictly a question):

> Tell me about . . . (the issues which are of vital importance for this project)

Open questions are good at getting people talking. They are also useful for probing further into an answer which wasn't quite full enough the first time round.

Closed questions start with the following words or phrases:

> Was . . . (this an important feature?)
>
> Did . . . (you find the way here without trouble?)
>
> Were . . . (you able to finish on time?)
>
> Are . . . (you going to stay?)
>
> Is . . . (it a nuisance?)
>
> Could, would, do, fall into the same category.

These closed questions can be very useful. For example, if you want to find out whether someone smokes or not, it is much more effective to ask, 'Do you smoke', than, 'How do you feel about smoking' or 'What is your position about smoking?'. However, if you want someone to tell you about what they think or feel, open questions are more effective at starting off the process. You may well have dealt with people who when asked, 'Do you smoke?' actually gave you a lecture about how they felt about smoking and the logic, ethics and health issues surrounding it, but as a general rule, you will make life easier for yourself if you ask an open question when you want someone to talk about an issue and a closed question when you want a yes or no answer.

A good illustration of this is the panel game Twenty Questions. In it, celebrities are asked questions about themselves to which they are only allowed to reply 'yes' or 'no'. Sometimes the panel guesses who the celebrity is and sometimes they do not. If the panel was allowed to ask questions such as 'What is your job?' and 'What are you famous for?' they would guess their celebrity more quickly and accurately, though this would of course ruin the point of the game.

All questions are either open or closed. Let us now look at the way they can be used to turn them into helpful tools in any negotiation.

Less conventional questioning techniques

CHUNKING UP AND DOWN

Once you have asked a question you receive an answer. You may need some clarification of this answer. Perhaps you need to know the motivations or thoughts behind the answer. Perhaps you need to know the detail of exactly what the person has in mind. The type of question you ask will lead to the type of answer you receive. When we categorise or store information we tend to do so in chunks – whether we are storing it mentally or physically. When you give someone your telephone number, you probably do it by splitting it up into manageable chunks rather than a whole string of numbers. Chunking is a term borrowed from computer programmers. Chunking up means going from the specific to the more general, chunking down means going from the general to the specific or even more specific.

When you are negotiating, you will not always want to take at face value some of the statements made by the other person. Perhaps you want to know more of the background to their position, why they want what they want, what is in it for them or their team or organisation. This is where chunking up can help. Chunking down is useful where you need to know more factual, detailed information to fully understand the meaning of a statement.

121

CHUNKING UP

Some children at about the age of four, seem to use the word 'Why?' more than any of the others in their vocabulary. The bend in the Pembrokeshire road where my daughter was told about a bull which had escaped from its field, still evokes memories of the interrogation which followed on and off, but mostly on, for the next four days. A child does not ask 'Why' necessarily to receive an explanation, but to be able to relate one fact to another fact that she understands. 'Why' is a question which tries to expand an idea so that you can see what is behind it. If you ask 'Why', you often get a reply in terms of the big picture rather than the detail on the picture. For example the question 'Why do you want to take a year off to travel?' is likely to get the type of reply: 'To see the world/ find myself as a person/have a good time'.

However, 'Why' is a question that some people answer with 'I don't know' or 'I just want to'. There are two ways around this.

1: Just leave a silence while they work out the answer to why.
On a radio programme recently a young man was asked why he had agreed to keep a diary of what happened to him as he went through a

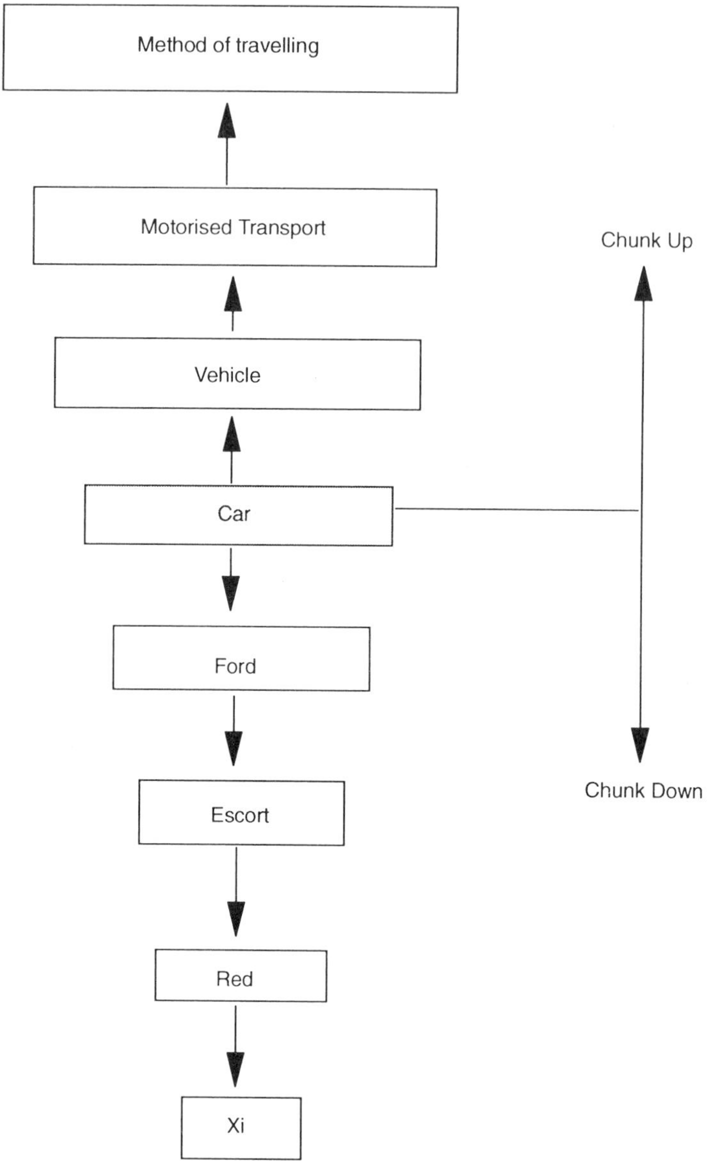

Fig. 10.3 Chunking up and down

period of great change in his life. His answer went something like this.'I don't know. I really don't know,' (silence). 'I don't know, – I suppose because I think the step I'm taking is important and I want people to see what is involved in it.'

This young man had not previously articulated his reasons for agreeing to participate. He did not have the reasons in his conscious mind. As he talked, he came up with a reason, almost seeming to talk himself into it. It may or may not have been the real reason, but it was the asking of the question and the silence which followed it, which stimulated the thought process.

2: Ask a better question.

'What will doing X mean to you?' or 'What will having Y do for you? are both questions which help the answerer to articulate the real 'Why' in a clearer and more focused way. If the young man on the radio programme had been asked 'What will keeping a diary heard by millions mean to you?', he might have been able to express his reasons in a way which gave a clearer indication of his real feelings about the issue.

If you ask: 'What will doing X mean to you' and get the answer, you can chunk up again by asking a similar question. Let us go back to our round the world trip example.

> *'What will taking a year off to travel do for you?'*
> 'It will mean that I see many different countries.'
> *'What will seeing many different countries do for you?'*
> 'I'll be able to experience lots of different cultures and see things I know nothing of at present.'
> *'What will seeing many different cultures mean to you?'*

123

It is possible to see how this conversation could go many ways at any of the answer points. The questioner here is *chunking up*, getting above and behind the stated reason for taking the year off. This technique can be important in negotiating, because if you ask the question of yourself, it can help you clarify the real reasons for your desired outcome. If you ask it of the people you are negotiating with, it helps them focus more clearly on their desired outcome and you both to identify other ways in which you could move jointly towards it.

Just as 'Why?' can be extremely irritating when asked over and over again, it is necessary to be careful not to sound repetitive with your questioning using this technique. Vary the questions:

> 'What will that do for you?'
> 'And what will that mean?'
> 'How will that affect you?'

so that the answerer doesn't feel hounded or interrogated.

CHUNKING DOWN

If you want to know something specific about the travelling year off, you will have to ask a specific question, for example:

'What do you want to achieve?'
'What do you want to see?'
'What are your reasons for going?' etc.

Chunking down means getting at the detail, unpicking the generalisations, distortions and deletions which creep into everyday conversation. This sort of question pinpoints precisely what might be the source of the problem and seeks to clarify it.

'I will prepare for the meeting'
'How specifically will you prepare for the meeting?'

'I need a large reduction before agreeing'
'Exactly how large a reduction are you talking about?'

'You will have to make some concessions before I can agree'
'What specific concessions did you have in mind?'

QUESTIONS TO CHALLENGE ASSUMPTIONS

Some of the most infuriating words in the English language are those that limit people in some way. Some of the words such as 'can't' and 'must' are self-limiting, others such as 'should', 'ought' and 'never' have value judgements hanging round their necks. You can challenge the self-limiting and value laden assumptions these words cause with one simple question: 'What would happen if I/ you/we did (or didn't)?'

'I can't find time to do this extra work'
'What would happen if you did?'

'We must get there in time'
'What would happen if we didn't?'

'You shouldn't ask favours of people'
'What would happen if you did?'

'Everyone has to clock in on time'
'What would happen if they didn't?'

The answer to any of these questions may be a factual one – but it may be a question which does make the other person pause for thought. If you did the extra work, you might gain insight, promotion, interest, or you might have to give up something else which would be no loss. If you didn't get there on time, perhaps you would miss the match or perhaps nothing very dreadful would happen. If everyone didn't have to clock in on time, perhaps they would be more self-regulating and motivated.

QUESTIONS TO DEAL WITH GENERALISATIONS

You are quite likely to meet the generalisation in negotiations. The situation where someone has a bad experience once and turns that into an expectation that things will always or never be like that. A single defeat in a race is turned into 'Everyone can run faster than me'. Failure to get a report in on time becomes, 'Harold never gets his reports in on time'. The mention of work not properly completed may become, 'The boss is always picking on me'.

In everyday life, generalisations may be irritating but unimportant. In a negotiation they can be a real obstacle to progress, because they can distort perceptions enough to change attitudes or to entrench positions. You can deal with generalisations very easily, by repeating the specific generalisation in a questioning tone of voice.

> '*Everyone* can run faster than you?'
> 'He *never* gets his reports in on time?'
> '*Always?*'

As in the last example, repeating a single word can be an effective antidote to unhelpful generalisation.

The creative use of questions in negotiations

125

QUESTIONS TO ESTABLISH THE BIG PICTURE

Establishing the big picture means getting behind the stated objective to a higher level outcome. Why does person A want to achieve outcome B? What are his reasons? What lies behind his seemingly intransigent insistence that B and only B is what he needs? Chunking up is the most useful type of question for getting the big picture, because this type of question can help you to understand motivations. What are John's reasons for wanting to buy a bulldog? What will it mean to him? What will opening a new branch in Rotherham do for the Managing Director?

QUESTIONS TO GET OUT OF STALEMATES

When you have reached a stalemate,the chunking up question is one which can lead the way forward. Apart from helping you to understand motivations, a chunking up question can also help to discover the real concerns behind someone's unwillingness to drive to Cardiff on Friday. Asking, 'What would driving to Cardiff on Friday mean to you?' might bring out from the woodwork all sorts of anxieties, interests or problems about which you had no knowledge.

What if . . . questions are another useful tactic in a stalemate. You can use What if . . . to suggest another vision for the future, to help the other person to see what might be possible or available if they could or would agree to do what you want. If you are asking Nancy to drive to Cardiff on Friday and she is resisting the suggestion for many different reasons, ask What if . . . to help her to see what the outcome might be if she *were* to go, rather than concentrating on all the reasons why she can't go.

A stalemate is effectively a blockage. Some questions can help you to move around the blockages even if the blockage itself cannot be removed. In this case, you are trying to find out what would have to happen for the blockage to not be a problem.

> 'What would have to happen for the delivery date not to be a problem?'
> 'What would have to happen for Alex to agree to this plan?'
> 'What would have to happen for you to feel it way a safe way to proceed?'

QUESTIONS TO CLARIFY DETAIL

These are often called Probing questions – the sort of question you ask when you need more detail than an original answer gives you.

> '*How much* money is required?'
> '*How do you feel about* the move?'
> '*What do you mean* when you say that it would be unwise?'
> '*How do you mean?*'
> '*In what way?*'
> '*Could you explain that a little more fully?*'

Chunking down questions are also useful here.

> '*How specifically* do you want to do it?'
> '*What precisely* will it mean?'
> '*How exactly* do you want to proceed?'

QUESTIONS TO STIMULATE THINKING OR PUT OVER A VISION

Questions can be used to stimulate thinking for yourself or in others. Those which move thinking on or expand the range of thought are those which introduce some element of imagination or visualisation. For example:

> 'What if we were to introduce a completely new system?'
> 'How would it be if we decided to look for a different route?'

QUESTIONS TO GAIN COMMITMENT

At the summarising stage, or when trying to come to agreement, questions are often more acceptable than bald statements or demands. In everyday conversation, people use questions as a polite form of making requests and suggestions. Why drop the politeness when negotiating? 'Will you bring me that file please?' is unlikely to be answered, 'No, I won't', but is often more acceptable than 'Bring me that file please'. For example:

'Shall we ensure that both our managers are in full agreement to this?'
'Do you agree that this is an essential issue?'
'So you are happy to do this if I agree to do that?'.

The observant might notice that this last example is not strictly a question, but is a statement turned into a question by your tone of voice.

QUESTIONS TO ASK FOR FEEDBACK

Useful questions to use when asking for feedback about what you have done or said are:

'What is your view?'
'How do you see it?
'Are you happy with . . .?'.

QUESTIONS TO FLOAT AN IDEA

If you are unsure about how someone may react to a suggestion, putting it in the form of a question can be a useful lead in. For example:

'How would you react to the possibility of a merger between our two teams?'
'What if we started off by looking at the X before going on to the Y?'

Questions to avoid

There is really only one sort of question to definitely avoid when you are negotiating – the *leading* question. A leading question leads the respondent to give you the answer you are expecting. Avoid it for these reasons:

1 It can mean that you are given the obvious answer, not the true one.
2 You may lose a huge amount of information you would have been given if you had asked a straightforward question.
3 It makes you vulnerable to manipulation by the unscrupulous.
4 It can sound patronising and arrogant and can antagonise the answerer.

Some examples of leading questions are:

127

'I'm sure you agree that the most important issue is quality?'

'You check all despatches of course?'

'You are able to match our delivery deadlines aren't you?'

Making conversation with questions

There is an art to asking questions in such a way that it seems like a conversation, not an interrogation. Most of the art lies in the non-verbal behaviour of the questioner, such as tone of voice and facial expression, but much is also to do with listening skills – the reflecting back sort of question which rephrases a fact or feeling and uses it to encourage the speaker to go on talking. Softening your questions can make them less of an interrogation. Phrases such as, 'I'd find it useful to know . . .', 'Would you mind telling me . . .', or 'I wonder what it would be like if . . .' are softeners which have the effect of making a question less stark.

The ability to ask questions in a conversational way is a useful skill to polish for negotiating. You don't have to wait until you are negotiating. You can practise next time you need to make polite conversation with someone at a function or business meeting. Try using questions for the various purposes described in this chapter and surprise yourself with the quality and quantity of information you are able to collect.

Questions as a response to conflict

If someone comes storming into your office, ranting and raving about the shortcomings of yourself, the department or the organisation in general, you have a choice of ways to respond.

(a) You can rant and rave back, allowing their anger or aggression to infect you. This is particularly tempting if you are the subject of their wrath. It often leads to an escalation of the issue into a full scale row.

(b) You can adopt a calm and soothing approach, trying to pour oil on the troubled waters. 'Calm down, John' you might say. This carries the danger of transferring John's wrath from its original subject to yourself, for being so irritatingly unfeeling about John's obvious distress and anger.

(c) You can defuse their anger by asking factual questions, such as, 'What is the problem?', or 'What has happened?'. It is difficult to carry on shouting while answering factual questions. Once people start the pattern of stating facts in answer to questions, they begin to calm down. The very fact of stopping shouting to answer the questions means that the level of adrenalin falls.

It is extremely important to ask factual, non-threatening, innocuous questions, designed to elicit the details of the event which caused the outburst. The defusing of anger means that the escalation of minor conflict and friction into more serious conflict, can be avoided.

SUMMARY

Questions are so infinitely serviceable throughout the negotiation, from inaugurating the proceedings through to concluding the agreement, that they deserve to have a much higher profile than most negotiators accord them. Once you have mastered the basic techniques of asking questions, you can go on to get the detail you require, find out the motivations behind statements, encourage creative thinking, break stalemates, float ideas, and gain commitment. These are really only a few ideas for the uses of questions – once you feel comfortable using them, you will find many more ways to employ them. Use the following checklist to begin to extend your use of questions.

Checklist

129

1 Be aware of the deletions, distortions and generalisations which abound in everyday conversation.

2 Avoid unnecessary mind reading.

3 Use open questions to open up a subject and closed questions to get a Yes or No answer.

4 Chunk up to get motivations or thoughts behind a statement.

5 Chunk down to find out more factual detailed information or fully understand the meaning of a statement.

6 Use questions to challenge assumptions such as 'can't', 'must', 'should' etc and generalisations such as 'everyone', and 'always'.

7 Use questions creatively in negotiations to:
   – find out what is behind stated objectives
   – get out of stalemates
   – probe detail
   – stimulate thinking or put over a vision
   – gain commitment
   – ask for feedback
   – float an idea.

8 Avoid leading questions, they only lead you into trouble or poor information.

9 Adopt a conversational approach so that your questions don't seem too much like an interrogation.

10 Use questions to defuse anger and avoid conflict.

11

Thinking: developing a rapid response mechanism

Have you ever been in a situation where you have solved a problem, dealt with an obstacle, or overcome a predicament to the best of your ability, maybe being a little unsure if it really was the best answer? Then later on, someone makes a comment, or you have an unbidden flash of brilliance which provides a much better answer, so that you think, 'I wish I'd thought of that at the time!'

We tend to get into habits of thinking, patterns which influence the way we evaluate ideas and make decisions. Some of these are very necessary for the minor decisions we make every day such as whether to have cereal or toast for breakfast, but sometimes the fact that we have got into habits of evaluating and decision-making can be a hindrance when we need to think fast in order to solve a problem. If you are going to be able to think rapidly when you are negotiating, you may need to make some adjustments to the way you have become used to thinking, so that you allow yourself to invent ideas more easily and creatively. This chapter will look at ways to put aside some of your habits of thinking and break out of the conformities which can inhibit your natural creativity. We will look at:

- Creative and analytical thinking
- Barriers to creative thinking and how to overcome them
- Techniques of creative thinking, including:
  - reframing
  - visualisation
  - worst consequence approach.

Creative and analytical thinking

Some of the thinking we do comes naturally to us. When we think without purpose, our thoughts don't necessarily follow one from the other in a logical order; they dart about. One idle thought may prompt another, ostensibly totally disconnected. When we dream, our dreams are often totally inconsistent and absurd. When we reason out a problem however, our thinking has a tendency to become more logical, to move from fact to conclusion in an orderly way.

ANALYTICAL THINKING

When children go to school they are taught to think logically. In most subjects, but especially maths and science, they are taught to reason from fact to conclusion. This type of thinking is called Analytical Thinking. It is *convergent* in that it takes a collection of facts and by eliminating various options, narrows down ideas to one solution. The process of logical thought leads to few or unique answers. This type of thinking is also called *vertical thinking* because there is one logical route which leads to the right answer and is illustrated in Fig 11.1.

ANALYTICAL THINKING

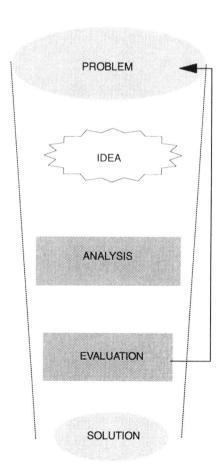

Fig. 11.1 Analytical Thinking is *convergent* and *vertical*

This convergent, vertical, analytical thinking involves deep and perhaps narrow probing to identify all aspects of the problem which need to be considered or eliminated.

CREATIVE THINKING

Creative thinking, on the other hand, is not immediately concerned with looking for solutions. Instead, it looks for many ideas which may lead to possible solutions. Creative thinking is *divergent*, in that it goes in many different directions to look for possibilities, and *lateral* in that it may go in a direction which appears to go sideways to, or around the issue, rather than straight to the point.

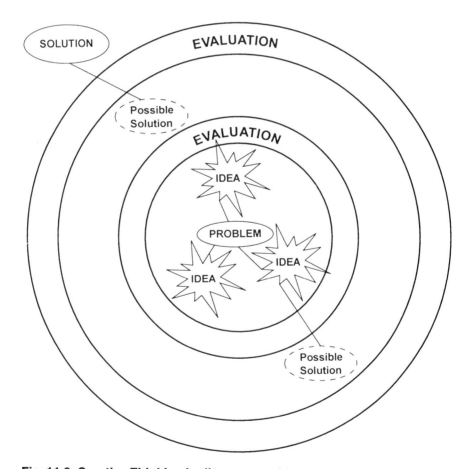

Fig. 11.2 Creative Thinking is *divergent* and *lateral*

This divergent, lateral, creative thinking involves a wide-ranging examination of all possible options, sometimes including the wild or foolish, or those which appear to be outside the problem and not linked to it. Many people tend to be better at analytical than creative thinking, especially when it comes to problem solving, as this is the approach they have been taught to follow. After all, it seems to be a much more reasonable and sensible approach. However, we are all *capable* of creative thinking. There are occasions when it is more effective to take the lateral, divergent approach, as the constraints of analytical thinking can fool us into believing that there is only one answer. When negotiating, we may come to believe that 'the answer' is not one which can satisfy everyone and that may be the time to take a more creative and lateral approach.

A nice example of creative thinking, is the reaction of the Ordnance Survey when their plan to remove redundant triangulation pillars caused mass protest from walkers who were fans of 'trig points'. Their bright idea was to allow anyone interested to 'adopt' a trig point, the adopter becoming responsible for the upkeep, painting and general welfare of it (with various constraints applicable against too much customisation). Instead of dissent and rows, they now have an enthusiastic response from walkers anxious to take on the responsibility, while the trig points remain the property of Ordnance Survey.

133

BARRIERS TO CREATIVE THINKING

Barriers to creative thinking have often been built up so effectively that we are not aware that they exist. In order to become more effective creative thinkers, we need to identify the barriers so that we can find ways of moving them aside or climbing over them. Those we look at here are:

- patterns
- fear of looking a fool
- dominant ideas
- tethering factors
- polarising tendencies
- boundaries
- assumptions.

PATTERNS

People like patterns. We tend to fall into patterns such as always putting the same leg in the trousers first or sitting in the same carriage on the train everyday. Have you ever set off to drive somewhere with your head full of plans or worries and found yourself instead on the road to work? 'The car knows its own way there' you say, but what you mean is that when your conscious mind lets go, your unconscious mind drives the car in the pattern it usually goes. Having a pattern doesn't necessarily mean that you do the same thing over and over again, but that you know what to expect. One thing is likely to lead to another, predictability is the order of the day.

A patterning system is very useful as it allows you to carry round your own personal map of the environment. It allows you to attach labels to things. For example, you may think that John is a reliable worker. John is establishing a pattern so that in the future you will know what you mean by reliable, and whether or not Jim and Joe live up to that label.

In the same way that people have patterns of behaviour and patterns of speech, they have patterns of problem solving. Most of the time these patterns work very reliably. However, if creative thinking is needed for a problem, then the comfortable and familiar patterns people have established for themselves can make it difficult to look for a different pattern. The patterns which might stop you thinking creatively are:

Expecting the obvious

One of the classic examples in creative thinking is to look for the answer to $1 + 1 = ?$ Most of us, without thinking (because the answer is obvious) would say 2. Imagine that you are not allowed to have the obvious answer. What could the answer be then? Look for the answers at the end of the chapter.

In a similar way, if you want a new video recorder and you don't have enough money, the answer may be obvious. The difference here is that the obvious answer may be different to different people – to one person it may be obvious to buy a video recorder on credit, to another it may be obvious to do without, to another it may even be to break into a likely looking house and help himself to one which belongs to someone else.

This tendency to look for the obvious answer is one reason why creative thinking can sometimes be essential in negotiating a settlement which can satisfy more than one person. If I am negotiating with you, and the obvious answer to me is one thing and the obvious answer to you is quite another, perhaps we both need to start wondering what other answers there may be to $1 + 1$.

When there does appear to be an obvious answer to a problem, it is tempting to adopt that solution without further ado and waste no more time and effort on it. Having a solution seems to be the important thing and there is often a reluctance to challenge the obvious answer to see if it is the best one.

Conformity

Where a pattern exists in organisations, many people are afraid to diverge from it. Patterns of behaviour are established and the unspoken rule is that people will conform to them. Patterns of influencing and of negotiating are formed as well as many others. The House Rules may be unspoken but they certainly exist. These patterns are being recognised more often these days and often earn the name of Company Culture.

The Automatic No

A new idea might automatically be rejected, even without thinking about it, maybe because the idea comes from a junior member of staff, or another department, or someone outside the team. This may be particularly noticeable in negotiations because you may automatically be tempted to say 'no' to an idea which comes from someone who is not on your team. So if you have an idea about the way forward which means the other side have to change their approach to a problem, remember that you may need to help them to see the idea for themselves – if you put it across as your idea for solving their problem it may get the Automatic No.

135

Linked to this is the question:

'Why don't we/you . . .'.

This question is actually *inviting* the Automatic No. It's asking for the reasons why something should not be done – and it usually gets them in no small measure.

Evaluating too quickly

Every one of us has an in-built capacity for evaluating ideas and making decisions, which we use instinctively when ideas are put forward. One problem which can occur is evaluating too quickly. The idea, 'What about shipping some of our supplies by canal?' may get responses such as, 'That's silly', 'We've tried that before' or 'That won't work'. The built in evaluating system dismisses the idea without giving it proper consideration. The idea and the evaluation of it are almost simultaneous – and the idea may not even be spoken before we have evaluated it out of court without the chance of a fair trial.

How can we get away from evaluating too quickly? One method is to separate ideas very firmly from the evaluation of them, a process which is formalised in brainstorming. When properly run brainstorms take place, it is mandatory that *no* ideas are evaluated. Every idea is written down, however silly, petty, boring or downright illegal they may be. When the flow of ideas is finally exhausted, *then* they are evaluated. Another way of avoiding the instant evaluation is by asking some questions, such as, 'What would be the benefit of shipping part of the supplies by canal?' 'How would it work?' etc.

FEAR OF LOOKING A FOOL

Professional comedians like people to laugh at their jokes, but if their personal affairs make the headlines and become the butt of other people's jokes, that's a different matter. The two-year-old will deliberately behave in ways which make his grandparents laugh and call him cute, but if they laugh when he is making a serious attempt at something, he will become angry and frustrated. No one likes to be laughed at unless they are intending to be funny.

Fear of looking foolish is one of the barriers which prevents people putting forward ideas which they think may be thought wild or silly. There are also strong barriers to going against the culture of the organisation and the way things are usually done. Many managers tend to be fairly conservative and to be tentative about challenging universally accepted views and practices.

Edward de Bono, one of the best known proponents of lateral thinking, suggested five other barriers to creative problem solving in *Lateral Thinking for Management* (1971).

DOMINANT IDEAS

'We tried our best to negotiate with them, but they seemed to be talking a different language.'

A dominant idea organises the approach to the problem just as a dominant person may organise a group. For example, in discussing the problem of congestion on motorways, the dominant idea may be the need to keep increasingly large numbers of cars and lorries moving along at reasonable speeds. Because this is the dominant idea, various solutions have been proposed including building extra carriageways, limiting junctions, creating toll roads. The dominant idea is to make travelling easier for large amounts of traffic, and the solutions are geared to this dominant idea. Other less powerful groups may of course have other, more radical, dominant ideas about congestion on motorways, which might involve reducing the number of cars or imposing stricter speed limits. Their dominant ideas will therefore produce different types of solution.

It's fine to have a dominant idea as long as you recognise it as such. You may also need to recognise that other people may have a different dominant idea from yours. If you are negotiating, having a different dominant idea to your opposition means that you may be operating from a completely different premise from them. It's the sort of occasion which may cause you to say, 'They were talking a completely different language.' By that you don't mean that they were talking French, Spanish or Russian, just that their dominant idea was different from yours, so that you were approaching the problem with completely different perspectives on it.

Tethering factors

A tethering factor is one which is always included in an approach to a problem, for example that the higher up the management ladder you go, the more you should be paid. Or that if you use more of a commodity such as gas, electricity or telephones, you should pay more for it.

The Conservative Party got into dreadful trouble when they tried to apply a different tethering factor to local taxation. The tethering factor that everyone had become used to was that the richer you were, the more you should pay towards local taxation. This was measured by the size of house you lived in, so that the bigger the house, the more you paid in rates. With most political parties agreeing that the system of rates was unsatisfactory, they went about changing the system. However, they didn't just change the system, they changed the tethering factor. They used the tethering factor that every person should pay an equal amount for the services they used such as refuse collection, policing, schooling etc. The outcome was the Poll Tax – so universally disliked and reviled that it was one of the first things a new party leader was anxious to change, especially in the run-up to a General Election. The point is that whether or not you think the Poll Tax was a fair system, it was a different way of looking at *fair* from the way it had been operated in the past.

When you negotiate, if you make it obvious that you are using a different tethering factor or encourage others to acknowledge their tethering factors, movement from either side can be facilitated. Once tethering factors are removed or recognised, a lot more opportunities or possibilities may be revealed.

137

POLARISING TENDENCIES

A polarising tendency is seeing something in terms of black or white. We can either do it this way or that way. All too often in negotiations it becomes a matter of, we can do it my way or your way. It is limiting because it suggests a choice between two extremes.

BOUNDARIES

Boundaries are the limits within which a problem is usually considered. There are always circumstances which govern the way we work or conditions which have to be met. Usually, you look at the problem within the limits of the circumstances such as time, number of people involved, importance of task etc. Sometimes these boundaries are vague or undefined and we may question them, but even where boundaries seem to be well defined it can sometimes be useful to ask, 'What if the boundary was not there? What difference would that make to the way I approach this problem?'. Doing this has the following effects:

- it may enable you to find a way to move the boundary in some way

- it may enable you to become clearer about what it is you actually want

- it may enable you to find another way to achieve your objective without moving the boundary

- it may cause you to question whether the boundary is a real boundary, or one which is self-imposed or unnecessary.

ASSUMPTIONS

Assumptions are a necessary part of life. We could not get through our lives without making daily assumptions. We assume that shops will open when they say they will, that trains will normally run, even if not on time, that if we turn up for work and do a reasonable job, we will be paid at the end of the month.

Making assumptions can be dangerous in many ways when you are negotiating. We have looked at some of these ways in other chapters. Here we are concerned with looking at how assumptions can stifle your creative thinking. Some assumptions are valid, some are not. When you are trying to think creatively, it doesn't matter if you make an assumption *as long as you know that you are doing so*. So if you are assuming for example that the council has given you all their reasons for wanting to dig up the road outside your office on the very day when you had arranged to move to an office up the road, that's fine, *but be aware that you are making an assumption*. Check it out, there may be something else there that you don't know that could help you to think around the problem.

The biggest danger with assumptions is that they escape attention. You don't realise that you are making them. It's easy to assume that another company calculates their profits in the same way as you do. It's easy to assume that people will not want to work on Sundays. When you make assumptions, you are taking it for granted that everyone has a similar map of the world to yours. Finding out that they do not can free up your thinking and allow you to find answers which might otherwise not have occurred to you.

Tactics for thinking more creatively

Thinking creatively does not mean proving that existing ideas or solutions are wrong or inadequate and therefore looking for a better one. It means generating different ideas to see whether they could offer an alternative solution.

MOVING OR JUMPING THE BARRIERS

The simplest way to begin to think more creatively is just to be aware of the barriers we have identified. You can use various phrases or questions to stimulate yourself to avoid thinking within the tramlines which might have constrained you in the past. If you use these aloud, you may also find that they stimulate other people to extend their thinking. Some of the phrases or questions you can ask or tell yourself or others are:

'Forget about that for a moment . . .'
'What other ways might there be of looking at this?'
'What other options might there be?'
'If that constraint did not exist, what would we do?'
'That's an assumption. What would happen if we didn't make that assumption?'
'Do we need to take either of these positions?'
'That fact is probably true, but suppose it were not?'

139

REFRAMING

Reframing is a creative thinking technique which has become much more widely known in recent years. It is a technique which originated with Neuro-Linguistic Programming, but has become more and more used as a management technique for problem solving. You may well have come across it without realising it, as it does not always carry the label 'reframing'. One of the classic reframes which has been absorbed by a number of managers is: 'It's not a problem, it's an opportunity'.

What is reframing?

If you have a painting which is in a frame, you get used to looking at it in that frame. You are very familiar with it, you know what it looks like, you know what to expect when you look at it. If you take that painting out of its frame and put it in another one which looks quite different, you may get a completely different perspective on the painting. You may notice things about it that you haven't been aware of before, because you are seeing it in a new light.

A common example of reframing that many people use without realising it is to look at the rain which is spoiling the cricket match or school fete and say, 'Ah well, it's good for the garden'. What they are doing is taking the rain out of context and looking at it from a different angle. In the case of the school fete, the reframe does not actually help the event at all, but it might help you to feel slightly more positive about the rain.

You can use the same technique with problems. When you reframe a problem or a statement, you take away the old way of looking at it and find a new, usually more positive perspective. The reframe will not necessarily provide you with an answer to the problem, but seeing the problem in a new light may persuade you that you can do something about it rather than just suffer.

Problem: The new course on Leadership in Management was an absolute disaster. All the delegates were unhappy and it achieved spectacularly low ratings.

Reframe: We learned a lot about what delegates from that background did not like. We discovered what they found was not relevant and have a good basis for revamping the course.

Problem: There is not enough space in the office.

Reframe: The fact that we need more space means that we have expanded/are more successful/can afford to buy more equipment.

Reframing in negotiations

When you are negotiating, reframing can help to move things on, to break stalemates. If you get to the position where you cannot agree about a number of issues, reframe by looking at the issues on which you do agree, or reframe by looking at how well you have done to have sorted out so much of a complex problem.

Problem: My company needs to be paid more than £30 per tonne for a product in order to make a profit. Your company cannot afford to pay more than £28 per tonne.

Reframe: Both our companies have cash limits, which gives us something in common.

This reframe could be the starting point for looking at other ways in which money could be saved between the two companies. Could the buyer provide a service for the seller which wouldn't be too costly or too burdensome, thus making up the shortfall in per tonne payments? Could the seller take advantage of some of the buyer's expertise or advice to reduce costs perhaps? The process of reframing indicates a willingness to look outside the problem as presented. It is one of the ways to start the creative thinking process.

Look at the following statements and create as many reframes as you can for them. Some suggestions will be found at the end of the chapter, but they are certainly not exclusive.

1 The management college is not making a profit.
2 The tree is overshadowing the room and causing it to be dark.
3 There is not enough work for the number of people employed in the factory.
4 No one is willing to work overtime.
5 The price is too high.

Some of these reframes can give a starting point for a new approach to the problem. For example, *No one is willing to work overtime*, transformed into *Everyone is willing to work during core hours*, could be the starting point for thinking about how you could achieve the same productivity in core time as you would expect to get if some people did work overtime. Maybe you would be better off offering bonuses for high productivity, or if time off is what your staff value, extra holiday in return for harder work.

WORST CONSEQUENCE APPROACH

141

The worst consequence approach is another way of reframing a problem or solution. It is most useful when looking at different options, when you are not sure if a course of action would be useful or appropriate. If someone is dithering about whether or not to do something because they are afraid that it might go wrong. The question to ask is: 'What would be the worst that could happen?' Having identified the worst possible case, the next question is: 'Would it matter?'.

The answer will often be 'no'. If it does matter, the next question is: 'What would you do then?'. When people think about the worst possible outcome then think about what they would do if that happened, it often becomes an acceptable outcome, something with which they could cope.

It is one way of looking at the cost of not reaching an agreement. What would be the worst that could happen if you did not reach an agreement with the person with whom you are negotiating? It is also a good starting point for your thinking in how to reach your BATNA – your best alternative to a negotiated settlement.

In an insurance broker's office, I overheard a conversation between the broker and a saleswoman from a particular insurance company. The broker was complaining that the insurance company in question had increased premiums for the contents of buildings by 5 per cent. One client had two properties and had renewed his premium on one before the 5 per cent rise. He was now making a fuss about paying a higher price for the contents of the other property. The broker wanted a better deal from the saleswoman. He felt that 5 per cent was too high a price hike compared with other insurance firms offering the same service and was refusing to do any more business with her unless the percentage increase was reduced. The saleswoman was in a difficult position, because the 5 per cent rise was centrally imposed and she did not have the power to do anything about it there and then. She had to leave a very unsatisfactory situation, saying that she would have a word with X and would come back to him about it.

Talking to the broker afterwards, it was clear that he was quite determined not to do business with that particular insurance company unless they changed their policy on price increases. He had thought through the consequences of his decision. He had asked himself, 'What would be the worst that could happen if I stopped doing business with them?'. The answer had been that he would have to persuade some of his regular customers to change their insurance company at their respective dates of renewal. This would involve his staff in some extra work. Also, there might be a few customers who were not prepared to change and he would lose their business. Having thought about this, he had decided that he would be prepared to accept the worst that could happen in order to try to get a better deal for his customers.

Asking yourself, 'What would be the worst that could happen?', is useful when preparing for negotiating, so that you are clear what you would be prepared to accept. It can also be useful in the actual negotiation itself. You can ask the question, 'What would be the worst that could happen?'

- of yourself when preparing for the negotiation
- of yourself when your opposite negotiator makes a suggestion which does not initially seem feasible
- of your opposite negotiator when they are sticking on a particular point: 'What would be the worst that could happen if we *did* do it this way?'
- of all parties when stalemate is reached. 'What would be the worst that could happen if we did not reach agreement?'.

VISUALISATION

Visualisation means looking at what would happen if a particular course of action were to be followed. It involves imagining what life would be like if we did make that decision, or take that action, or avoid this issue. It involves asking the question:

'What would it be like if . . . (we did/didn't, we couldn't/could, etc).

Looking at unlikely outcomes

Visualisation can be used to look constructively at possible outcomes for actions which you might otherwise not consider, or to help other people to do so.

> Statement: 'We cannot consider raising the price of our products to customers.'
> Question: *'What would happen if you did?'*

The answer to this could obviously be very varied, but some examples of the reply might be:

- people would carry on buying it because they like it
- some people would buy a different brand
- they would expect a larger quantity/better quality
- we would have to advertise a lot to show people why our product is better
- customers would expect something different
- people might think it is better quality because it is more expensive
- most people would still buy it because they cannot get anything comparable at a similar price
- it would depend how much we raised the price, and so on.

143

When you look at and verbalise the possible outcomes, some of them might not seem as instantly dismissable as they did originally. Would it matter if some people bought a different brand? (Depends on how many you think 'some' might be). Would it be feasible to give customers something different, or slant your advertising towards emphasising quality, which might encourage people to buy despite or perhaps because of the price rise?

Making a better choice of options

Visualisation can be used to think through various options and make a better choice.

Problem: You are negotiating the deadline date for completing a project. The project team leader has come to you and said that they need an extra month in which to complete the project. You have to decide whether to allow them some extra time or to insist on completion on time – otherwise you will invoke a penalty clause.

What would it be like if you did give them the extra time?

Answers might include:

- they would do a much better job
- it would give them the time to check all their facts
- they would think you were an easy touch and never meet a deadline again

- they would respect your ability to be flexible.

What would it be like if you didn't give them extra time

Answers might include:

- the quality of the finish will not be good
- they will just have to work harder and longer to get it done
- it won't be finished to the required standard
- it won't be finished
- there might be problems working with this team in the future.

These answers are just some of the many which might be true for that situation. When you are in a position like that, and you ask yourself *What would it be like if. . .*, you have a fairly good chance of making an accurate assessment of the outcomes. Even if you don't, you have widened your thinking about the problem which might have set you off on the trail towards an acceptable solution.

Breaking the habits of a lifetime

Breaking habits of analytical, vertical thinking and beginning to think more creatively is the first step towards being able to think on your feet to better effect. It takes a while to forget the old habits of analysing problems and to learn new habits of looking outside and around as well as straight ahead. So it's worth practising thinking creatively whenever you have a problem to solve, not just when you are negotiating.

Practise reframing, visualising and the worst consequence approach. Practise asking yourself questions about the barriers you might subconsciously be raising. Think broad, not narrow. By no means abandon analytical thinking – sometimes it is very necessary, but *add in* creative thinking to your repertoire of decision-making and problem-solving approaches.

Use this checklist to help you overcome some of the barriers to creative thinking and begin to develop a rapid response mechanism.

1 Check to see if you have fallen into a pattern of thinking. Are you:
   – expecting the obvious?
   – conforming to an established way of doing things?
   – using the Automatic No?
   – evaluating too quickly?
2 Are you stopping yourself from taking the risk of thinking creatively from fear of being unorthodox and perhaps being thought foolish or odd?
3 Have you made allowances for other people's dominant ideas – that they may be approaching a problem with a completely different perspective on it from yours?

4 Have you identified any tethering factors – factors which are 'taken for granted' which may be limiting your ability to take a completely different approach to the problem?

5 Check the boundaries to the problem. Are they really where they seem to be? Do they really exist in the form they seem to take?

6 Check your assumptions. Do you know that you are making them and are they valid?

7 Ask questions to check on other people's dominant ideas, patterns, tethering factors, boundaries and assumptions.

8 Reframe problems when you can. Take a look at a problem from a completely different side of the picture and see if it looks any different.

9 Look at the worst that could happen. What would happen if it did?

10 Visualise different outcomes to problems. Ask 'What would happen if . . .', 'What would it be like if . . .', to help you and others think through and clarify various options and outcomes.

Answers to creative thinking puzzle

$1 + 1 = 11$ or X or L or V or T or = or > or <
using all the symbols, including the $+$ and the $=$, many other answers are possible.

Suggestions for reframes

1 The management college is not making a profit.

Reframes: (a) It gives the staff a better insight into how managers in unprofitable or threatened organisations feel
(b) It is the perfect opportunity to examine current practices and see what needs to be changed
(c) It's a chance to see how costs might be cut now and in the future
(d) It means they have to take a hard look at why business is not as good as it could be – this could improve their products and service.

2 The tree is overshadowing the room and causing it to be dark.

Reframes: (a) It's a beautiful tree
(b) It makes the room cool and shady
(c) The room needs lightening up (this is refocusing attention from the tree to the room)
(d) It prevents strangers peering in through the windows from the street.

3 There is not enough work for the number of people employed in the factory.

Reframes: (a) We have enough people to take on extra work
(b) We still have work for some people at the factory

4 No one is willing to work overtime.

Reframes: (a) Everyone is willing to work during core hours
(b) We have the opportunity to offer work to other people on a part time basis.

5 The price is too high.

Reframes: (a) The price is high, so someone must be prepared to pay for it
(b) I don't want to/can't afford to pay that much for it
(c) As the price is so high, have I missed anything about the quality etc of the product?

12

Dealing with the unexpected

Wouldn't it be nice if everything went as planned? If the person on the other side of the table had read the same negotiating book as you had, and knew exactly what you were trying to do and how he should respond? If you could guarantee that people would react in the way you expected them to?

Sadly, life's not like that. Despite your best endeavours, sometimes the unexpected will happen. You will have to deal with situations which you had not anticipated. Sometimes people will not play the game according to your rules – and their rules might be outside your experience. Unforeseen events are those where thinking on your feet is perhaps most essential. You need to be able to react rapidly but effectively. In this chapter, we look at some of the unexpected phenomena which you might come across when you are negotiating and at ways to help you to cope confidently and successfully with them. We look at:

- fear of the unexpected
- unexpected opposition
- unexpected proposals or ideas
- unexpected cooperation
- unexpected negotiation situations.

Fear of the unexpected

When you feel nervous before you start negotiating, stand up to make a speech, start to do something you haven't done before, the butterflies in your stomach are there for one of two reasons.

> You don't know what is going to happen next
> *and/or*
> You are afraid of failing in one way or another.

The two are closely linked because if you don't know what is going to happen, you don't know whether or not you can handle it. Even if you do know what is going to happen – you are going to stand up and make a speech – and you have rehearsed it and got it more or less perfect, you may be afraid that something you are not expecting will cause a disaster – your voice may disappear, or you may trip over the podium and land flat on your face.

So fear of the unknown and fear of failure are closely bound together. This means that when something unexpected happens, it can cause us to think less clearly than usual because we have a slight shutdown of mental capacity caused by mild panic. Susan Jefferson, in her excellent book *Feel the Fear and Do it Anyway* suggests that the only fear which really matters is the fear that you won't be able to handle whatever happens. If you believe that whatever happens, you will be able to handle it, then you will be able to cope with anything unexpected which life, or the negotiator on the other side of the table, throws at you. So the first step is to control the riot beginning in your brain by telling yourself, 'I CAN HANDLE THIS'.

THE CRITIC ON YOUR SHOULDER

If you can train your inner voice to give you more positive messages, you will be able to deal with all sorts of problems more easily because it will be easier to get into an appropriate state of mind to do so. So what sort of changes need to be made?

Change   'I'll never be able to cope with this'   into
          'I can cope with anything I put my mind to'

Change   'You've really got yourself into a mess
          this time'   into
          'You can get yourself out of this mess'

Change   'You stupid idiot, look what you've done now'   into
          'How are you going to use your skills to sort this
          out?'

You will be familiar with the sorts of messages your inner voice sends you. Think about the ways you could change them to make them more positive. Turn the critic on your shoulder into the mentor and friend on your shoulder, and notice what a difference it makes. Having a trained and friendly inner voice can be particularly useful when you are faced with unexpected opposition. If your inner voice is sending you the message, 'Well you didn't expect that, but you can handle it', you will be much more likely to react positively than if your inner voice is telling you that this is the final straw and that you had better throw in the towel and go home now. When you meet with unexpected opposition during a negotiation, let your inner voice say to you: 'Don't panic, ask a question'.

Unexpected opposition

1 You are explaining to one of your colleagues the plans you have made for allocating certain pieces of work. You believe you have made a fair distribution of the workload, dividing up equitably the interesting and not so riveting. Suddenly she says 'No, I don't want to do that'.

2 You have negotiated long and hard and believe you are within range of reaching agreement. Your opponent has been reasonable and willing to move towards you, in exchange for some movement on your part. You have one final point to clear up, small but important. Your opponent refuses to budge one inch.

3 You go to your boss to ask her approval to sign up for a training course, expecting her to sign and wish you luck. She refuses to let you go.

4 You make what you consider to be a perfectly reasonable suggestion when negotiating with another department about budgets. Instead of responding positively, their representative says, 'Trust you to think of that – that's (personnel/marketing/sales/etc) all over.'

149

KEEPING YOUR COOL

Unexpected opposition can sometimes be felt as a threat. We often react to a threat by becoming defensive or angry. In most cases, little is gained by reacting defensively or by expressing your anger at unexpected opposition. If you become defensive,the other person may perceive it as an attack and become aggressive themselves. If you become angry, you may well be less effective at expressing your opinions and feelings. So you need to keep your cool. Do this by:

1 The old favourite, count to ten.

2 Think about the state you would like to be in. How do you want to feel? Calm? Relaxed? Able to handle anything? Remember the sensation of feeling like that. Then tell yourself, 'I want to feel calm'.

3 Think of a reframe – it will take your mind off your anger.

Reframing

Reframing is a technique which has been dealt with in a lot more detail in the chapter on thinking. Briefly, reframing enables you to look at a problem from a new angle. By doing so, you often get a new and more positive view which enables you to adapt your approach, rather than be restricted by the confines of one view.

Original statement	Reframe
'She refuses to give in on this point.'	'She may have another idea about this.'
'He won't budge.'	'He has moved a long way already.'
'She won't let me go on the course.'	'She is giving me the opportunity to practice negotiating.'
'He's attacking my department.'	'Here is a chance to find out what he really thinks about my department.'

GAINING TIME

When you run into unexpected opposition, your first reaction is likely to be shock. It might be so fleeting that you would hesitate to call it shock, but there will be a momentary stop in your reactions which may prevent you from being able to respond immediately. The severity of the shock will depend on just how unexpected or vigorous the opposition is. Some of the phrases we use to express our reaction to unexpected events or opposition, show that we perceive it as a force which has the power to stop us in our tracks.

'You could have knocked me down with a feather.'

'I was bowled over.'

'I was frozen with horror.'

Because the shock has the effect of momentarily numbing your responses, the first thing to do is to gain time. You may want to try some of the following:

1 Express the fact that the opposition was unexpected and that you need a bit of thinking time: 'I wasn't expecting you to disagree, I need a moment to think about that', or 'That's a bit of a shock, I'm not quite sure what to say at the moment, let me just think about it before I give you an answer'.

2 Repeat their statement of disagreement back to them: 'You say you don't want to do that'. This has three benefits:

(a) When you repeat their statement, you are not using your brain to have to react, you are gaining some time by making a response which needs no thought by reusing their words and at the same time confirming that you have understood what they have said.

(b) You may get the straight answer, 'That's right'. By this time, you may well have given yourself enough moments to begin reacting to their statement. If not, you can fall back on expressing the unforeseen nature of their statement.

(c) Sometimes, the repetition of their phrase acts as a question, so that they give you an explanation of the reason why they don't want to do it. This gives you a lot more thinking time as well as a lot more information on which to base your reaction.

QUESTIONS

Our old friend the question will once again be your greatest ally in dealing with the unexpected opposition in your negotiation. Perhaps the one which will leap immediately to mind, to be asked in an indignant and bewildered tone of voice is: '*What do you mean*, (I can't go on the course/ you're not prepared to negotiate about that/ you don't agree to the plans)?'

This may not always have the desired effect. This question and its derivatives, is an expression of your hurt or anger or shock. It may sometimes elicit a reasoned and rational explanation, but it is just as likely to trigger defensiveness on the part of the other person.

151

What do you actually want to know at this point? You want to know the *reasons* for their refusal to do what you expected. So the obvious question to ask is:

'What are the reasons for that?'

You may want to phrase this in different ways depending on the circumstances, but that is the basic information you are seeking. By asking the question, you are also re-establishing dialogue between you, beginning the process of negotiating about that point. Following on from that, you can go on to ask all sorts of other questions, already mentioned in other chapters, such as 'What if', 'How', 'What about' and so on. The starting question, 'What are the reasons for that?', will get you out of shock and into negotiating again.

Unexpected proposals or ideas

When you prepare for negotiations, you sit down and work out what you want and how you might be able to achieve it. You also think about what you imagine the other person might want and what they would be prepared to bargain with. Usually, you have a reasonably good chance of being near to the mark, even if your predictions of their agenda are not perfect. Occasionally though, someone will come up with a proposal or idea which is completely outside the scope of anything you envisaged. It may be unconventional or startling, or it may just stretch the parameters of the discussion further than you had expected.

Humans have a finely tuned system for assessing and evaluating which tends to favour the familiar and expected and is biased towards rejecting the unexpected or out of the ordinary. So that if someone makes an 'outrageous' suggestion, the automatic response tends to be 'No'. This Automatic No response also tends to be applied when an idea comes from someone else, not from ourselves. If a friend asks your advice, and you give it, you will often get into 'Yes, but . . .'. It goes like this:

'I don't have enough money to make ends meet, what shall I do?'
'You could take on another job in the evenings.'
'Yes, but I'm tired after my day at work.'
'You could let out your spare room to a lodger.'
'Yes, but I don't like having other people around and . . .'
'You could sell your flat and move somewhere cheaper.'
'Yes, but . . .' and so on.

The suggestions given above are not necessarily brilliant ones. They are ideas coming from outside the person with the problem. So the person with the problem puts his energy into looking for reasons why they *would not* work rather than putting his energy into thinking for himself of ideas which would work. How do you avoid falling into this trap? When someone comes up with an idea which doesn't immediately strike you as the answer to prayer, how do you stop yourself thinking, if not saying, 'That won't work'?

APPLY CURIOSITY

As children, we are naturally curious. We want to know why wheels go round and what is in that cupboard and what we would look like if we cut off all our hair. Slowly we are taught to curb this natural curiosity. 'It's rude to stare', 'Don't be nosy', 'Stop asking silly questions'. When faced with an unexpected idea or proposal, dust off that natural curiosity and bring it out of the cupboard. Ask yourself and any others around:

'What would it be like if we did that?'
'What might happen if we tried that?'
'How would that work?'

By doing so, you are giving yourself the opportunity to visualise and sound out the possible outcomes of applying an idea. You may be able to get a feeling for what might happen if you were to take the idea further. Applying curiosity stops you rejecting ideas out of hand. It means that you are prepared to consider other people's ideas even though at first they may sound ridiculous or unworkable.

LOOK FOR EVIDENCE

Applying curiosity is the first step. Following on from that, you need to find out a few facts. Remember, you need to check out that you have understood what they mean. Don't make the assumption that your interpretation of what John said is the same as his interpretation of it. Take one sentence of John's. You may have a good idea of what he means because you have the same background knowledge as he does, but look how many places there are where misunderstanding could occur if you don't check your understanding of his meaning by asking him to be more specific about what he means.

'I suggest we set up *a number of project groups* to take *responsibility* for the *different components* of *this scheme.*'

a number of	– how many spring to your mind?
	– is it the same number as he has in mind?
project groups	– what does that mean to you?
	– does it have the same meaning for him?
responsibility	– what is your interpretation of this word?
	– does he interpret it in the same way?
different	– what do you think the components are?
components	– what does John think they are?
this scheme	– do you both perceive the scheme as the same?

So let us look at John's sentence again. 'I suggest we set up a number of project groups to take responsibility for this scheme.'

Firstly, apply curiosity. What might it be like if you did? When you do this, you put your own interpretation of John's sentence to the test. so the next step is to ask him to explain his idea more fully, so that you have a better picture of what he feels the outcome would be. Then you may need to do a little probing. What exactly does he mean by project groups? What specific responsibilities does he suggest that they have? Which specific parts of the scheme does he envisage handing over to them? When you do this, you are not only clarifying John's idea for yourself, you are finding out just how well he has thought it through. If it was an idea off the top of his head, you may be helping him to examine just how well it would, or would not work.

BE ASSERTIVE

If a criticism is unexpected, inappropriate in the circumstances, or mistimed, suggest assertively that the middle of a negotiation may not be the best time to deal with the issue. Suggest another time when the matter concerned may be tackled more appropriately.

Unexpected cooperation

The unexpected doesn't always have to be nasty. Sometimes pleasant surprises occur – even in negotiations. Occasionally, you may gird yourself up for a tussle, if not a fight, and be taken aback when the person you were expecting to oppose you welcomes you with open arms, or at least gives in without a struggle.

ACCEPT GIFTS GRATEFULLY

Some unexpected cooperation is genuine, straightforward and above board. If it is a simple case of the other person accepting your complaint, point of view or proposal because they recognise it as valid or necessary, take their cooperation gratefully. Don't fall into the trap of saying 'Are you sure?'. If you do, you may find that suddenly they are not sure!

WHEN NOT TO ACCEPT GRACEFULLY

Sometimes, the situation is not as clear cut. You may have had very good reasons for supposing that you needed to negotiate long and hard about an issue and find it difficult to understand why the other person has unexpectedly cooperated with you. It may be difficult to decide when to challenge their cooperation or agreement. On the one hand, you may not want to remind them of an issue they might have forgotten. On the other hand, if you simply accept their willingness to collaborate, you may go away from the encounter still unhappy about the outcome for a number of reasons.

1 *Suspicions*. You may be suspicious of their motives. What were their reasons for doing what you wanted? Do they know something which you don't? All sorts of questions may wake you up in the night, as you wonder why it was all so unexpectedly easy.

2 *Ethics*. If your outcome is to achieve the best outcome for both parties, you may be less than completely satisfied with an outcome which gives you what you want, but does not seem to be beneficial to them.

3 *Perfectionism*. If you get a result which satisfies you, you may still ask yourself if it is the best result you could have achieved. Perhaps discussing and negotiating the matter would have enabled you to come up with an even better result – better for you as well as for the other person involved.

CHECK FOR CONGRUENCE

Use your skills at establishing rapport to test out how genuine the cooperation is. Observe any slight changes in muscle tension. Match their posture and their tone and pitch of voice. Listen, look and feel for incongruity. Does what they are saying match what their bodies are telling you? If not, say so. 'You seem to be agreeing with me, but I don't feel sure that you really mean it.'

EXPRESS YOUR FEELINGS

If you decide that you do want complete openness, so that you avoid suspicions or worries about how good or how ethical the result was, expressing your feelings will help to clarify things. Be open about the fact that you are surprised or pleased or shocked at their cooperation. Be careful to do this in a way that is not a put-down nor a victor's shout of triumph. Do an internal check of your motives – do you want to allay suspicions, achieve the best result, or just check that you have actually got the facts straight? Say something like:

'I'm pleased you agree. I was expecting to meet with a little more resistance . . .'
'I'm happy we've come to an agreement. Can I just check, . . .'
'I'm pleased to settle that so quickly. I am a little surprised though, that . . .'
'I'm glad you are happy with that. Before we finalise the decision, can I just ask . . .'

155

CHECK YOUR UNDERSTANDING AND SUMMARISE AGREEMENT

When cooperation is unexpected, check that you have all your facts straight. Check that you have really grasped the meaning of what they have said. If you do not, you run the risk of accusations and recriminations later. The reason for the unexpected agreement may just be that you and they have different interpretations of the same situation, or that you have misunderstood their approach. So test your understanding of the facts and summarise what you understand to be the agreement by saying something like:

'Can I just go over what we have agreed and check up that we have both got our facts straight?'
'I'd like to make sure that we are both certain about what we have agreed . . .'

The unexpected negotiation

Imagine the scene:

1 You are walking along the corridor, with your head full of the January sales figures, and Claudia stops you and says that she wants to have a

word with you *now* about coming off the Analogue project next week.

2 You are peacefully mowing your front lawn when your neighbour pops his head out of his front door and suggests that you should pay for repairing his greenhouse as he is sure that the damage must have been caused by your son's football.

3 You are working, your way through your in-tray, when your boss appears and says that as you have all the facts and figures about xyz, she wants you to go and negotiate a deal with the supplier as Nigel is off sick today.

There will be many occasions at work and outside of work, where you may find yourself suddenly precipitated into a situation which calls for your negotiating skills. On some of these occasions, you may be able to buy yourself a little time in which to prepare, others may require you to perform instantly.

Earlier in this book, preparation has been held up as one of the prerequisites of a successful negotiation. So how are you going to manage if you don't have any time to prepare? Does this mean that you are bound to fail? Not necessarily, although negotiating on the spot is never very easy and often the outcome is not as satisfactory as if you had had time to prepare.

GAIN SOME TIME

Wherever possible, acquire a little extra time. It may not be very much, but any thinking time is better than none. You may be able to put off the encounter for an hour or so if you ask: 'Can you give me an hour to think about this?'. Or you may need to be a little more subtle or devious in acquiring a small amount of thinking time. 'Let me just (put these papers down/turn the lawnmower off/close this window/etc) before we start.'

When all else fails, go to the lavatory. No one ever denies you the time to go there, nor (with the exception of your nearest and dearest perhaps), questions the time you spend there.

HAVE AN INSTANT, LIMITED OUTCOME

Whenever you negotiate, it's important to know what you want to achieve. When you are faced with a situation where you have to negotiate unexpectedly, you won't have time to think deeply about your outcome, and all the ramifications which could be involved if you were to make this decision set that limit. How can you ensure that you have an outcome which will be a satisfactory one, even if you haven't had long enough to think about it properly?

Limit your horizons. Ask yourself, 'What do I want to achieve *at this meeting*?'

Your outcome may be to show your willingness to negotiate, then adjourn until you have had time to do more preparation. For instance, in the examples given above,

1 Your outcome here may be to find out why Claudia wants to come off the Analogue project. She may then be willing to have the rest of the discussion later.
2 Perhaps your instant outcome here is to stay on good terms with your neighbour, or to find out exactly what has happened to his greenhouse and why he feels your son played an active part in that happening.
3 We could be talking about either of two negotiations here. One is negotiating with your boss about whether or not you should take Nigel's place, the other is the negotiation with the supplier.

When negotiating with your boss, your instant outcome might be to gain some time, or get some help, or get some more information. When negotiating with a supplier, your limited outcome might be of a different kind. Perhaps you would limit yourself to negotiating that part of the business which it was essential to do that day, and arrange for the rest of it to be continued at a later date.

157

GET THE WHOLE PICTURE

When you are dropped into a situation where you need to negotiate, your questioning skills need to jump up and show their worth. It is particularly important to ask a lot of questions so that you are aware of the whole background of the circumstances. You need to get into your head a rough idea of the picture in the other person's head.

- what is their outcome?
- why is it important to talk about it now?
- what specifically do they want to achieve?
- how specifically do they want to go about achieving it?
- what are the burning issues for them?
- what are the less important, but still relevant, issues?

If you have been thrust into the negotiation with little notice, it is quite reasonable to ask a number of questions before putting your own point of view. You can preface the questions by saying something like: 'You'll appreciate I haven't had much time to think about this, could I just ask you one or two questions to start with, to help me get my thoughts straight?'.

SUMMARY AND CHECKLIST

In this chapter we have looked at how to cope with the unexpected when you are negotiating. Wheel your rapid response mechanism into practice rather than panicking by confronting your fear of the unexpected and acknowledging that you have the knowledge and skills to cope. Make sure you have an inner voice which encourages rather than criticises. Move towards handling the unexpected competently and confidently by using the checklist below.

1 When faced with unexpected opposition:
  (a) Keep your cool by – counting to ten
  – controlling your emotional state
  – reframing the situation
  (b) Gain time by – asking for thinking time
  – repeating or reflecting what they said
  (c) Ask factual, non-confronting questions.

2 When faced with unexpected proposals or ideas:
  (a) Avoid falling into the trap of 'Automatic No' by:
  – applying curiosity
  – looking for evidence.

3 When faced with unexpected cooperation:
  (a) Accept gifts gratefully
  (b) Don't accept without question if:
  – you are suspicious of their motives
  – ethically, you are not satisfied with the outcome
  – it is not the best result which is achievable
  (c) Check for congruence between words and non-verbal signals
  (d) Express your feelings – surprise, pleasure etc
  (e) Check your understanding and summarise agreement.

4 When faced with an unexpected negotiation:
  (a) Gain some time
  – put it off for an hour
  – do a minor chore (e.g. open window)
  – when all else fails, go to the lavatory
  (b) Have an instant limited outcome, limit your horizons
  (c) Get the whole picture.

13

Moving through stalemates

Jack was negotiating with his neighbour about replacing the fence between their two properties. The current fence was a lapboard fence, very dilapidated and shabby, through which Jack's dog escaped to go on private adventures. The fence was actually Jack's, but because of the layout of the gardens, his neighbour saw more of the fence than he did, because Jack had a shed and a greenhouse along that side of the garden. Jack was happy for the fence to be chain-link fencing which was cheap, dog-proof and needed no maintenance – it had been hard to get behind the greenhouse and shed to put wood preservative on the old one.

Jack's neighbour was unhappy about Jack's proposal to put up a chain-link fence as he thought it would look ugly. He was not unhappy with the current lapboard fence as it was covered with climbing plants on his side. If the fence had to be replaced at all, he wanted another of the same kind, so that he could grow plants against it on a trellis. The cost of a lapboard fence was twice as much as of a chain-link fence. Jack asked his neighbour to pay for half the cost of a lapboard fence. His neighbour said that while he was willing to make some contribution, he felt that half the cost was too much. Jack felt that paying more than he needed, just to keep his neighbour happy, was not a workable solution.

So what do you do when you've moved as far as you think you can, and the other person in the negotiation won't move?

Stalemates seem to be fairly common in the negotiations which reach the public eye. In fact, most of the negotiations that reach the national or international news get there *because* they reach stalemate. During 1993, every time the news was switched on, there seemed to be yet another negotiation which had broken down – the French fishermen couldn't agree with the British over fishing waters, the teachers couldn't agree with the government about tests for 14-year-olds, the railworkers couldn't agree with British Rail over the wording of an agreement over possible redundancies and proved it by going on strike on more than one occasion. Most tragic of all, the warring factions in what was Yugoslavia couldn't agree to the Owen – Vance Peace Plan. That list is only a short selection of the negotiations which came to public attention which had 'broken down'; reached a point at which the parties involved were unable to move close enough together to come to an agreement. When examples like these seem to be the norm for negotiations, it's no wonder that many people become worried at the thought of negotiating – it is seen as an event which is likely to end up as a conflict.

We have already looked at how you can prepare in order to achieve a solution rather than a stalemate, and the strategies and tactics you might use to avoid them. However, if despite your best efforts, the negotiation you are carrying out begins to look as if it might be heading for a stalemate, there are some things you can do to keep matters moving.

AVOID STALEMATE TURNING INTO DEADLOCK

In negotiating, stalemate is when you have come to a point where nobody can offer any other ideas, giveaways, concessions or whatever, to help move the two parties towards a settlement. Deadlock on the other hand, is where neither party is prepared to move any further at any price, in fact, the very idea of doing any sort of deal together begins to look repugnant to them.

It pays therefore to use all your skill and imagination to move yourself and the other person out of stalemate as fast as possible. But how do you achieve movement when it seems as if both parties have moved as far as possible? In this chapter we look at some techniques to stop the stalemate turning into deadlock and to help you kick-start the stalemate back into negotiation. There are three stages to this:

- first reactions
- evaluation
- creative ways forward.

AN IMPORTANT NOTE ABOUT QUESTIONS

In both these stages, the use of questioning skills is crucial. Stalemate occurs when two parties have become stuck – they cannot move with the data available at that time. Therefore, new data is needed to remove the glue. Most of the steps and techniques discussed in this chapter involve the thoughtful and skilful use of questions to expand the area to be explored to make a way out more available.

First reactions

- apply a mental icepack
- sort out your thoughts
- look for common ground

APPLY A MENTAL ICEPACK

To avoid stalemate turning into deadlock, the first step is to take a cool calm and collected look at the situation as it stands now and the history of it's progression to that point.

1 Deal with your emotions. Isolate yourself from any feelings of irritation, disappointment or anger which may have been stirred up by the stalemate.

2 Isolate the reasons for the stalemate – there may be more than one. Is it to do with them, you, or a combination of the pair of you?

SORT OUT YOUR THOUGHTS

Having dealt with any emotions surrounding the issue and applied a mental icepack, your general frame of mind can make a vital difference. The way that voice in your head reasons, can make the difference between continued movement and the breakdown of communication. If you begin to think:

161

'This is never going to work'
'She really is an intransigent old fool'
'We're never going to agree on this one'
'I really don't see how I'm going to get him to move on this one'
'This looks like the end of the road'
'There isn't anywhere we can go from here'.

then you are confirming for yourself that you have come to the end of the negotiation – almost talking yourself into it in fact – and the next stage is conflict or surrender.

There is another way. It doesn't come as naturally, and may need some working on at first, but if you can turn your mental voice into a positive and forward-looking entity, it's the first step in preventing stalemate turning into deadlock. Your thoughts this time are along the lines:

'We can make this work'
'Why is she being obdurate?'
'How can we reach agreement on this one?'
'How can we move out of this sticky patch?'
'Where do we go from here?'

LOOK FOR THE COMMON GROUND

One of the first steps to take to resolve a stalemate is to look for common ground. What have you agreed so far? Or if you haven't agreed on anything, what do you have in common? If two parties come together to negotiate, they must have *something* in common – even if it stops at the recognition that they have a problem.

Evaluation

■ summarise agreement so far
■ look for the positive
■ work together to find a way forward
■ look underneath.

SUMMARISE

1 What you have agreed so far.
2 Your respective initial positions.
3 Your original reasons for negotiating.

Summarising what you have agreed so far, where you have come from, the progress you have made, has a number of effects. It jogs your memory, reminds the other person of what has been discussed and lays the situation on the table for a fresh look, giving you a clear point from which to move on.

Take a fresh look at the reasons why you are negotiating. Sometimes in the heat of discussion, it is easy to lose sight of the overall outcome – why you are engaging in this pastime in the first place – and the negotiating becomes a game which both parties want to win. What do you want to achieve? What do they want to achieve? Bringing these questions back to the forefront of both parties' minds can help to recreate movement.

An organisation moved out of an office building after twenty year's tenancy. When they originally took on the lease they had signed a document agreeing to return the building to its original condition at the end of the tenancy. In fact they had made a number of alterations to the building, including putting in suspended ceilings and an air-conditioning plant. All these were now at the end of their useful life. However the building was now twenty-five years out of date and it seemed obvious that before it could be relet, the landlord would have to carry out a complete refurbishment.

The landlord knew that a complete refurbishment would need to be made and preferred that instead of refurbishing the building, the tenant should pay a substantial sum in compensation, but as a bargaining strategy, was prepared to insist that if the money was not paid, the building should be returned to its original state.

The negotiations became heated, neither negotiator was prepared to give way. The tenant's representative felt that they were morally if not legally in the right in suggesting that as the landlord needed to refurbish in any case, they should not need to contribute towards this. The landlord's representative insisted that it was £200,000 or do the work themselves.

The two parties needed to go back to looking at what they had in common and what they wanted to achieve. They found that:

(a) The common ground was that they needed to find an agreement to the problem.
(b) The landlord wanted to achieve a large contribution to the refurbishment of the building and compliance with the tenancy agreement originally signed.
(c) The tenant wanted to achieve a cheap way out of their legal obligations and a recognition of the apparent logical and moral basis of their case.

Once they had both recognised at this late stage that they did have some common ground around which they could agree, and that the desired outcomes of each could be reconciled they were able to start moving towards each other. They did so by an analysis of the various computations each had made about the cost of refurbishment and some bargaining around that. Eventually they came to an agreement that the tenant would pay £80,000 towards the cost of the refurbishment.

163

Looking from a safe distance, this sort of solution may seem obvious. However, in the heat of the moment, it is not always so easy to divorce oneself from moral and legal rights, until one goes back to asking, 'What is it both parties actually want to achieve? How can they move forward together so that each attains at least part of it?'. In the above case, the settlement of the bill became lost in the argument about the rights and wrongs of the situation, until, by summarising, the two parties were able to look again at their desired outcomes.

LOOK FOR THE POSITIVE

Look for the positive in the other person's position and encourage them to look for the positive in yours. Focus on the things you have in common, things you have agreed so far. Tell the person with whom you are negotiating about the aspects you think you have in common – if nothing else, this will include the need to get the deal done. Also tell them what you think you have achieved so far and what you have agreed so far. Now get them to tell you about the positive features they can identify. Use questions such as:

'What do you see as our areas of agreement so far?'
'What common ground do you think we have identified?'

If they remain negative, you may need to be more specific and directive in your questioning:

'Do you agree that we both need to sort this out before Tuesday?'
'Are we agreed that the delivery schedule is one of the most vital areas?'

Every time they say 'Yes' to agreeing with you, you are focusing them on the positive. Yes is a positive word.

WORK TOGETHER TO FIND A WAY FORWARD

You don't have to do this alone! You can make an assumption here. If George is negotiating with you, presumably he has a reason for doing so. He must need to get something out of the negotiation. So rather than try to get out of this stalemate by yourself, involve George in resolving the problem. One of the issues you might raise is:

What will happen if you don't reach agreement?

Bring out into the open the gains you will achieve from reaching a solution, and take a clear look at what might be the outcomes if you do not. Examine in some detail the options open to you both if you do not reach an agreement.

If you have planned beforehand what you will do if you do not reach agreement, say what it is. Say why you would prefer to reach a negotiated agreement. Ask them what they will do if they cannot reach an agreement with you. You may often find that they have not thought this one through, which should give them an even better reason than yours to want to reach agreement.

WHAT'S UNDERNEATH?

Address their concerns

Look for what might be behind the other person's refusal to move. What might be their concerns, needs or fears.

Andrew was a trainee in a pensions department. He knew that it was the organisation's policy to allow staff to have day release to pursue qualifications which would be useful to them at work. He applied through the proper channels for day release to do a DMS – Diploma in Management Skills. His manager turned him down on the basis that the qualification was not directly relevant to the work he was doing. Andrew really wanted to do the qualification and went back to the manager with evidence of how he and the department could benefit if he was allowed to do it. The manager said that he was not convinced that the benefit would make up for the time which would be lost by Andrew doing the course, and that in his opinion it would be better to become really good at the job and achieve promotion and recognition by that route. At this point Andrew had three choices:

1 He could surrender and give up the idea of doing the DMS this year at least.
2 He could fight – get the staff association or union on his side and take his grievance to higher authority.
3 He could try to resolve the stalemate by looking behind the refusal of his manager to what might be the manager's underlying concerns or motives.

The sort of questions he might ask could be;

(a) 'What problems would it cause you if I were to do this course?'
(b) 'What specific benefits can you see from me learning on the job rather than having day release?'
(c) 'Is there any reason in particular why you don't want me to do this?'
(d) 'What other information do you need to be convinced that it would be useful for me to do this course.

In fact Andrew took the third course, looking for the reasons behind the refusal, and it turned out that his manager had two concerns – first, would Andrew become too big for his boots and try to tell his superiors how to manage once he got some information about how it was supposed to be done, and second, how the work would be done in time if he lost Andrew for one day a week. Andrew was then able to suggest that he should try doing the course for one term because he was convinced that his extra motivation and the occasional extra hour would allow him to get the work done – he offered to work an extra hour on three days a week if necessary. The very fact of his boss stating his fear about Andrew becoming too big for his boots made it less of a problem – Andrew was warned of the concern and in the future his boss would be able to address it if he felt it was becoming a problem.

165

Why are they stalling?

Sometimes stalemate occurs because the person on the other side of the table does not have the power or authority to make the decision. If that is the case it needs to be identified as soon as possible so that something can be done about it. Questions are again your biggest ally: 'What is preventing you from moving any further on this one?'.

If lack of authority is the problem, the answer is to negotiate with someone who does have the power. You may have to arrange this in a way which allows your current opposition to save face, because he/she may not like to admit that they have to go to a higher power.

Is it a tactic? Are they stalling because they hope to achieve a better outcome for themselves by saying they cannot move any further when they can really? This needs to be nipped in the bud quickly. Some of the questions which might uncover this tactic are:

'How far do you have the authority to go?'

'I understood you had the authority to negotiate on this, what has happened to change the position?'

You may also need to issue a general reminder about the negative consequences of not reaching agreement. Stating the negative consequences of disagreement can sometimes be a very powerful force for moving away from stalemate. Humans are much quicker at moving away from pain than moving towards pleasure. If you are choosing your meal in a restaurant, you will be more careful to avoid the foods which make you ill than choose the food that gives you pleasure. You will pull your hand away more quickly if you burn it on the stove than you will move it towards something pleasant. However, if your negotiation style is full of threats and ultimatums, adding another one might have less effect than if your approach so far has been positive and cooperative.

Creative ways forward

- look at the bigger picture
- take a fly on the wall approach
- step into their shoes
- switch on thinking.

LOOK AT THE BIGGER PICTURE

Chunking up and down

Chunking is a term borrowed from computing which means breaking bits of information up into pieces. Chunking up means finding the larger piece, chunking down means breaking the information into smaller pieces.

Chunking up is a particularly useful technique to break stalemates by finding out what the bigger outcome behind the stated objective might be. Let us use the example of two managers competing for the one extra member of staff who is to be taken on in the next six months. Both can make good and seemingly watertight cases for needing the extra member of staff to augment their team. Neither is willing to give way. In this case, the personnel manager has to make the decision about who gets the extra person. The personnel manager asks each manager 'What would having the extra member of staff mean to you?'. Manager A answers that it would mean that she would be able to relieve some of the pressure on her staff who were showing signs of being unable to cope with the pressure of work. When asked, 'And what would that mean to you?', she replied that it would mean that they would all do their work better, so allowing her department to work more efficiently. Manager B answered that it would mean that he would be able to complete project x by the deadline. When asked, 'What would that mean to you', he was able to answer that it would mean that he would receive recognition for being effective in the way he managed his department.

You can see from the above example, that the question could be asked a number of times to get at the real motivation for a particular outcome. Of course you have to be careful about how you ask the questions. If it sounds as if you are beginning an interrogation, you are likely to end up with a defensive reaction.

Some examples of chunking up:

'I am not happy at all about moving from our current premises'
Question: *'What would staying in your current premises mean to you'*

'It is essential that the price increase goes ahead'
Question: *'What would the increase in price mean to you?'*

The answers to these questions could give you extra information which allows you to start looking at other or extra ways in which you might pursue the negotiation. It might be an opportunity for you to increase the size of the cake by including extra ingredients rather than merely cutting up the existing cake.

167

Moving around the blockage

You can use your questioning skills to help people move around blockages which they may have created. Again, you are trying to find out what is involved in the bigger picture – to find their motivations, what is important to them. Two very useful questions to ask here are: *'What would have to happen for this not to be a problem?'* and *'Under what circumstances would you be prepared to give way on this'*. Both of these questions help the recipient to widen the focus of the issue. They encourage him to think about aspects of the issue which might not have been in his conscious area of thought.

THE FLY ON THE WALL APPROACH

Sometimes when you are involved in a situation, it is not as easy to see it clearly as if you were an outsider looking in. If you think about the arguments you may have observed between other people, on many occasions you may have been able to understand fully why they were quarrelling, because you could see what was the real cause of the argument. You may even have been able to see both sides of the argument clearly and found it difficult not to intervene to try to sort it out.

Now think back to the last heated disagreement you may have had. At the time, were you able to see the other side of the argument? Were you able to understand where the disagreement arose? Were you able to listen rationally to the facts? For most people, the answer to those three questions is likely to be a resounding 'No'. This also happens when you are negotiating. Sometimes you become so involved that it becomes difficult to see any other way forward than the one you have planned and have been pursuing all morning. Like a horse with blinkers, you have a narrow view of the way forward. In order to break a deadlock, one of the first steps is to remove the blinkers by allowing yourself to be less involved.

Put it on TV

Try this first in a situation where you are involved, but the outcome is not crucial.

Take a mental step backwards. Imagine that you are seeing the situation you are in on a television screen in the corner of the room and that you can see what is going on without being involved in it. Make the television screen a black and white one, and turn the sound low. Now look at what is happening on your television screen. From this distance, what is going on? What are the two or more parties involved trying to achieve? What is preventing them from reaching agreement?

Even if you cannot get insights into those questions, by putting the situation on TV, you have given yourself a chance to distance yourself from it and see it from a new perspective. By removing yourself mentally, you give yourself the chance to understand the facts without becoming involved in the emotions.

Now that you are removed from it, have a good look at your TV. Re-run the video of what has happened so far and look at it from this dispassionate distance. Analyse what has been going on. You may be able to see where things went well and where they started to go wrong, what worked and what didn't work. You may even be able to understand more fully where the other person is coming from and what is their real (rather than stated perhaps) direction of focus. At this stage you are looking for two things:

(a) the whole picture
(b) the other person's point of view.

You can now go on to look for two more things:

(c) what would you do if you weren't involved?
(d) what might be the outcome of a number of different proposals/ strategies for movement?

From your comfortable armchair, now have a look to see what you might do if you were not involved in this negotiation. What might be your next step, your next proposal, or your next strategy for movement?

Now run the video forward, and have a look to see what might happen if you were to carry out Plan A, Plan B or Plan C. Obviously you can't *know* what will happen, but from your knowledge of yourself and of the other person's reactions so far, you can probably make a pretty good prediction. It's useful at this stage to have a number of alternative strategies so that you don't get bogged down in the 'one true way' to success. There is no one true way – something slightly different is going to work best each time.

STEP INTO THEIR SHOES

While you were preparing for the negotiation you tried to put yourself in the place of the other person by thinking about what their desired outcomes, needs, available concessions might be. If you get to the position of stalemate, you should have a lot more information available to you by that stage. This is another opportunity to put yourself into the position of the other person and to understand the problem from their point of view. It may be helpful to do this if you have an adjournment. To do this most effectively means going beyond sitting and thinking about it. This is what you can do:

1 Imagine the person with whom you are negotiating sitting in a chair opposite you. See what they look like, hear their voice.
2 Move into that chair and temporarily put yourself into the place of that person. Be that person. Do not say to yourself, 'I think Janet would think . . .', say 'I am Janet and I think . . .'
3 As Janet, say what you think about:
   – the position at the moment
   – the negotiation so far
   – the person you are negotiating with (you)
   – what your concerns are
   – what you hope will happen next.
4 Move back to your own chair and think about the insights you have gained before you restart the negotiation. By moving into Janet's place, have you been able to see the situation with her eyes and therefore gain a better understanding of where she is coming from?

SWITCHING ON THINKING

There are some powerful ways to open up the brain out of its blinkered, one direction approach and explore new and previously unthought of country.

■ what if . . .
■ reframing

169

- worst consequence approach
- use metaphors
- use counter examples.

Some of these approaches have been discussed in the chapter on thinking, but it is worth summarising them here.

What if . . .

This is a way to help people visualise the outcome of something. When people negotiate, they usually come to the table with an idea of what they want to achieve. They may not have as clear an idea of any alternative, though possibly quite reasonable, outcome. They may believe that following a certain course of action will lead to a particular wanted or unwanted outcome and have difficulty moving away from that belief without a little help. The use of What if . . . in a question can open up the options. The sort of question you might ask is:

'What might happen if you did?'
'What if we were to open a new branch in spite of all the problems?'
'What would it be like if we cancelled the order?'

Reframing

Reframing means taking a subject out of its old familiar coat and seeing if it looks any different, more promising, less threatening, in a different one. Take a dog, whom you see stretched out by the fire, looking as if its only interest in life was food and sleep. Take that same dog, let loose in the cargo shed in an airport to look for drugs and you get a completely different perspective on the same animal *because you are seeing it in a different frame.* Look for reframes for your own approach and help other people find reframes for theirs.

Worst consequence approach

Looking at the worst that could happen (a) if agreement is not reached, or (b) if a certain course of action is followed, is another way of reframing a problem.

You should have looked at the worst consequence for yourself of not reaching agreement when preparing for this negotiation and working out your Best Alternative To a Negotiated Agreement (BATNA). Revisiting that and helping your opponent to do so can:

(a) remind you that you do have a plan for the eventuality of not reaching agreement, which in turn eases tension by reducing the amount of stress you feel

(b) focus other people's minds on exactly why they wanted to reach agreement with you in the first place.

The worst consequence approach applied to taking a seemingly risky step forward, can help everyone to realise that the worst that could happen might not be so very bad after all, or that it wouldn't have as devastating an effect as they imagined.

'We really cannot pay more than £10,000'
'What would happen if you did?'
'We would not be able to afford to do some other renovation work'
'And what effect would that have?'

This conversation helps to clarify the reasons for the stalemate and encourages the person concerned to re-examine issues which he may have thought were fixed. Perhaps the other renovation work is not as important as achieving agreement about this issue. Perhaps when you know the rest of the problem you may be able to suggest other ways of solving it. Once more you are adding a bit more spice to the ingredients and increasing the size of the cake.

171

Use metaphors

Metaphors are a powerful way of putting your message across. When you use a metaphor you are illustrating your point by telling a story. People like stories and respond to them. It is possible to understand a story on an unconscious level and apply it to the message you want to put across. Whoever originally told the story of the little boy who shouted 'Wolf!', has had their metaphor borrowed on hundreds of occasions since, as it is such a simple but effective way of illustrating the point that many false alarms will make everyone more likely to ignore a real call for help.

You can use a metaphor for yourself if you begin to feel depressed because you are not becoming a skilled negotiator as quickly as you would like. When babies start to walk, they do not suddenly get up off the floor and march across the room. First they practise standing while holding on to the table or Dad's leg. Then they stand without support. Then they take their first wobbly steps. Their walking improves very quickly, but at first they fall down a lot – and even when they have become proficient, they still fall down occasionally.

Use counter examples

We all have belief systems which are very powerful. If someone's desired outcome is based on their beliefs and values, it is difficult to shift. If you have come to a stalemate because moving in your direction would violate the belief system of the other person then using a counter example might be an effective way of moving forward. Laborde uses the example of the belief system that killing is never a solution to a problem, but if the only way to stop a gunman with his pistol at the head of your two-year-old is to kill him, suddenly killing as a solution becomes viable. One counter example is not going to destroy someone's belief system, but it might be the basis for some movement.

IF ALL ELSE FAILS FALL BACK ON YOUR BATNA

If all else fails, fall back on your BATNA. You decided in preparing for the negotiation what your Best Alternative To a Negotiated Agreement was, so be prepared to live with it. You may well find that if others see that you are determined to withdraw, they will suddenly become more anxious to find a way to agree after all, and any bluffing on their part suddenly stops. However, do not bank on this. The whole point of having a BATNA is that you really are prepared to do it. It is not a bluff.

SUMMARY

172

When you negotiate, you may from time to time come to a point where you can't move and the other person won't. This chapter has looked at ways to move on from this situation. Use the following checklist to ensure that you retain a positive, problem-solving approach, even when it seems that you have arrived at stalemate.

Checklist

1 First reactions
    (a) apply a mental icepack by bringing your emotions under check, then isolating the reasons for the stalemate
    (b) sort out your thoughts by ensuring your inner voice is positive
    (c) look for the common ground between you

2 Evaluation
    (a) summarise to give you a clear point from which to move on:
       ■ what you have agreed so far
       ■ your respective initial positions
       ■ your original reasons for negotiating
    (b) look for the positive in the other person's position and encourage them to look for the positive in yours
    (c) work together to find a way forward, they have a stake in this too. Look at the possible outcome if you don't reach agreement
    (d) look at what might be underneath their refusal to move further:

- address their concerns
- find out why they are stalling.

3 Creative ways forward
  (a) look at the bigger picture by using questions to find out the motivations behind the stated outcome and to help people think about the circumstances under which they might be prepared to move
  (b) take a fly on the wall approach to distance yourself from the situation in order to be able to see it more clearly
  (c) step into their shoes to see what the situation looks like from their side of the table
  (d) switch on thinking by using the What If approach, reframing, Worst Consequence approach, metaphors and counter examples, to explore creatively fresh and innovative solutions to the stalemate.

4 If all else fails, fall back on your Best Alternative To a Negotiated Agreement and finish the negotiation there.

173

14

Handling conflict

Two cowboys pace slowly down the road towards each other, watched from behind the saloon bar door or a convenient woodpile, by cowering townsfolk. They stop, draw and shoot. One falls histrionically to the ground.

This means of solving conflict is one commonly depicted in books and films, in similar if not exact repetitions of the above example. It seems to be a pretty final way of resolving conflict, but in fact, the only party likely to get any long-term satisfaction out of it is the undertaker. The short sharp shock (or shot), may not lead to lasting peace – the enemy disposed of in short order today may be resurrected by others with the same cause.

What part does an examination of conflict play in a book about negotiating? First, all negotiations start off from a background of some sort of conflict. It may be conflict of interests, conflict of needs, conflict of opinion. It may be so understated and amicable that the word conflict does not spring to mind in connection with it, but if there were no conflict, there would be no need for negotiation. If you both agree about everything, where is the need to negotiate? Second, negotiation is one of the most commonly used methods of trying to resolve conflict. It is by no means the only method, neither is it always successful.

In this chapter, we shall look at some of the reasons for and issues around conflict, then examine ways to make the negotiations which often accompany it more fruitful and constructive.

Causes of conflict in organisations

A production manager was concerned with keeping costs down and operating his plant in the most cost effective way. This involved making as few lines as possible, because diversification would mean that the machines would be idle while changes were made to allow for different lines. The sales manager in the same organisation was concerned to maximise his turnover. To do so, he wanted a wide range of products to offer to his customers. The resulting conflict between the two managers resulted in loss of production and nearly caused the company to cease operating.

This example, quoted by Taylor (1986), is a good illustration of the far reaching effects which can be caused by conflict within organisations which are not managed, nor handled constructively.

Salaman (1978), suggested that organisations tend to be represented as harmonious cooperative structures, 'happy families', where conflicts are seen as exceptional, usually arising from personality clashes or misunderstandings. He suggests that on the contrary, organisations are arenas for individual or group conflict where opposing people or groups fight for limited resources, career progress, privileges, professional values and other valued rewards.

Salaman's descriptions reflect what might be called the naive and realistic views of the extent and variety of conflict within organisations. It is pleasant to think of the group you work with as a 'happy family' with the only conflict being a personality clash now and then. Realistically though, there may well be conflicts of interests within that group and there are even more likely to be conflicts between that group and other groups within the same organisation. Although each of those groups is ostensibly working towards the same end – the stated objectives of the organisation, in actual fact they will each have their own sub objectives, which may or more probably may not, be compatible with each other.

175

Conflict between groups is very common, both within organisations and outside the working environment. Think for a moment about how many different groups there may be within one reasonably small workplace. Take an office which has to deal with the public as an example. There are the front office staff who have to deal with the public and the back office staff who do not. There are management and clerical staff, management and unions, old and new, skilled and unskilled. There may be teams to deal with different tasks.

Whenever there are groups, there is the potential for conflict. Handy (1983), quotes an experiment which divided boys who had no previous knowledge of each other into two groups and had them sleeping in different dormitories and carrying out different activities. The researchers found that 'healthy' competition between the groups turned into conflict very quickly. When they broke up the groups and tried to integrate them after the experiment, they found it was very difficult to dissipate the conflict and they were never wholly successful in doing so. The conflict arose only because they were different groups.

When managers are asked about the causes of conflict at work, some of the most common areas they report are:

- competition for limited resources
- differences in objectives
- misunderstandings
- personality clashes
- disputes over areas of responsibility or authority

- disagreements over methods
- lack of cooperation
- poor performance
- failure to comply with rules or policies.

It is easy to see that many of the above could lead to differences of opinion, competition, issues for negotiation, but why do they move from an issue which might be settled relatively amicably, into conflict?

CONSTRUCTIVE CONFLICT

Recently, ideas of constructive conflict have become increasingly popular. The view that conflict is unavoidable, usually caused by troublemakers and detrimental to the achievement of organisational goals has increasingly been replaced by the view that conflict is inevitable and can be a catalyst for change. Not only is it inevitable, but can be useful if used constructively. Conflict can be positive when it helps to open up the discussion of an issue or results in a problem being solved. It can increase the level of individual involvement and interest in an issue and help people discover their abilities.

Handy (1983), distinguishes between three distinct types of conflict. He describes them as three types of *difference* within organisations, calling them argument, competition and conflict. He suggests that argument and competition are potentially fruitful and beneficial, whereas conflict is harmful. If handled badly, both argument and competition can degenerate into conflict.

He describes argument as resolving differences by discussion, where the contribution of many different views can lead to a better solution and suggests two prerequisites for productive and constructive argument.

1 The group should have shared leadership and should have confidence in and trust one another. Members of the group need to be able to express their feelings as well as facts.
2 The issues need to be handled in such a way that objectives are clarified and the discussion focuses on known facts, the goals to be pursued and the methods to be used.

Handy suggests that competing is the other positive means of handling differences. Competition can set standards of best performance and motivate people to produce more and work to a higher standard. He suggests that competition is only fruitful if it is open. Closed competition, i.e., one person gaining where another loses, can lead to destructive conflict, whereas open competition, where for example the size of the bonus is linked to the amount of productivity, can increase output constructively.

One of the most crucial elements of this is not whether the competition is *meant* to be open or closed, but the perceptions of the people involved in it. This could be why many performance pay schemes, which are introduced with the best of intentions, with the aim of introducing a more objective and fair method of rewarding staff, flounder because the staff concerned regard the system as benefiting some but penalising most. Even though the system is intended and designed to be open and fair, it is perceived as closed and unfair. Much of the conflict which exists and flourishes within and outside organisations is not productive and constructive argument nor is it open competition. Some of the most common reasons for this are:

- lack of trust
- different perspectives
- individual approaches to handling conflict.

LACK OF TRUST

One commonly used training exercise involves giving two groups an exercise whereby if they choose red and the other group chooses red, they both gain marks. If both choose blue, they both lose marks. However, if one group chooses red and the other group chooses blue, the group which chose blue gains marks while the group which chose red loses marks. The objective of the exercise, clearly stated, is to gain a positive score. It is *not* to gain more marks than the other team.

177

The thing which becomes immediately apparent when observing this exercise is the lack of trust which exists between the two groups. They do not trust each other to play red. This often means that both groups play blue. An 'us' and 'them' mentality emerges. Part way through the exercise they have the opportunity to negotiate with each other. This does not always lead to an increase in trust. Lack of trust often leads to both groups failing to achieve the objective of the exercise.

This lack of trust between groups is often reflected back at the workplace. Because different groups do not have any knowledge of each other's objectives or viewpoints, they do not trust each other.

In September 1993, the world was stunned by the announcement that a peace agreement was to be signed between Israel and the PLO. Among the speculation by the media as to what it would mean, would it last etc, a news reporter asked one of the Norwegians who had been hosting the talks at which the peace accord was agreed how it had happened – what had they done differently? The Norwegian representative said that they had all been together for a couple of weeks, they had had breakfast, lunch and dinner together, they had walked in the garden together – and at last they had begun to trust each other. The trust was the difference that made the difference.

DIFFERENT PERSPECTIVES

People will have different perspectives not only of each other, but of the conflict itself, depending on the position they come from and the views they represent. It is not important whose perspective is right or wrong. The important point is that they are different. In a union versus management dispute, or a front office versus back office dispute, each party has its own wants, needs, beliefs and values. The failure of the other party to recognise any one of these will intensify the conflict.

INDIVIDUAL APPROACHES TO HANDLING CONFLICT

Elias H Porter (1973), suggested that individuals behave differently when handling conflict because they have different motivations behind their behaviour. He suggested that there were three true types, with most individuals being a mixture of these types but probably more inclined to one type than another. He distinguished between these types by colour, but if we call them the *hustler*, the *helper* and the *analyst*, it will help to understand the differences between them.

178

The *hustler* is the type of person who likes to get things done. He is assertive and enthusiastic in pushing ideas through. He doesn't necessarily want to be in charge, but given a goal to reach and the authority to make it happen, he will be very happy. His emphasis is on action, movement and tasks accomplished.

The *helper* wants his behaviour to be beneficial to others. He is concerned that people are taken into consideration when there is a task to be done. He will help if he feels that will benefit people; if he feels it is of more benefit to stand back and let people learn by their mistakes, he will do so.

The *analyst* is concerned with logic and order. She likes facts on which to base decisions and is less concerned with accomplishing the task or considering the people, than with making sure that everything is correct, in order and logical. She may well be assertive or helpful if this is necessary to acquire all the relevant information and put it into order.

You will probably be able to recognise parts of all these descriptions in yourself. Most people do. However, if you are honest, you may feel that you incline more towards one type than another. Porter suggests that typically, when in a situation where conflict arises, an individual tends to retreat towards the behaviour with which they feel most comfortable.

The first response of the *hustler* might be some form of challenge, designed to fight off the opposition. The *helper's* first reaction may be a desire to smooth things over, if necessary going out of his way to meet the needs of the other party. The *analyst* is likely to take refuge in a reiteration of the facts, the rules and the logic of the argument. When pushed to extreme limits in a conflict, the *hustler's* response is likely to be a fight to the bitter end. The *helper* in extremity will give in. The *analyst* will withdraw completely, breaking off all contact.

Destructive conflict

Conflict can be destructive when:

■ people begin to feel disgruntled, dissatisfied or demotivated
■ the conflict becomes more significant than the task in hand and people are distracted from dealing with important issues
■ it leads to people or groups becoming insular and uncooperative with each other.

You may need to deal with conflict:

(a) as an individual involved in a conflict with another individual or a group
(b) as a member of a group in conflict with another group or groups
(c) as a manager or other leader in the position of an arbitrator.

Within any organisation, whether it is a multi-national conglomerate or the committee of the local nursery school, there are common practices in dealing with conflict. Some of these are:

■ the application of existing rules
■ the design or formalisation of procedures, such as discipline and grievance procedures
  – confrontation
  – formal negotiations
  – informal negotiations
  – separation of contestants.

They are not always effective in that the conflict is not always resolved.

THE GROWTH AND DEVELOPMENT OF CONFLICT

How does a small difference of opinion, in some cases lead to open hostility and destructive conflict between two people or groups? A model which describes different levels of conflict makes it easy to see how conflict can escalate.

Levels of conflict

Level 1 Discussion Rational, open, objective

Level 2 Debate At this stage, people may start to make generalisations and look for patterns of behaviour. Slight distortions of others representations may creep in. The degree of objectivity becomes less

Level 3 Deeds The two parties show a lack of trust in the way they treat each other

Level 4 Fixed images A preconceived image of the other party is established. Little objectivity is shown, positions become fixed and rigid

Level 5 Loss of face It becomes difficult for either party to give in because to do so would entail loss of face

Level 6 Strategies Communication is restricted to threats, demands, punishments

Level 7 Inhumanity Destructive behaviour often begins. Groups begin to see each other as less than human. Murderous thoughts might creep in

Level 8 Attack on nerves Self preservation becomes the sole motivation. Individuals or groups prepare to attack and be attacked

Level 9 All out attack No way back except for one side to win and the other to lose. No quarter is given.

It is easy to apply the above model to different levels of conflict, from international wars at one end, through union–management disputes and group conflicts, to a dispute about the tidiness of your teenage daughter's bedroom. The higher the level to which conflict gets before it is addressed and dealt with, the more difficult it becomes to resolve it. If conflict is ignored or repressed, it will escalate. If it is acknowledged and constructive action is taken, it can be resolved and may turn out to be a positive force for change.

ADDRESSING CONFLICT

One manager when asked about his conflict handling methods said, 'I just tell them, stop that, or you'll be in conflict with me and then you'd better watch out'. This, though direct, may not be the most effective way of addressing and effectively resolving conflict! If you are involved in the conflict yourself, it may be more difficult to take a reasonable and rational approach, but the following steps can be used both by those involved and by those who may find themselves in the position of mediator.

1 Find out the facts
   (a) what is the real issue?
   (b) what is the history?

    (c) what is really going on?

    (d) who are the people really involved?

2 Identify the needs of both parties

    (a) own your own feelings (whether you are involved or not)

    (b) what do the people involved really want?

    (c) why do they want it?

3 Assess

    (a) is it a manageable size? If not, break up big issues into a series of manageable concerns

    (b) what level has this conflict reached? If it has escalated beyond level 3, more than one issue may be involved, so again you may need to divide it into bite-sized bits

    (c) can you do anything? If you become involved, do you stand a reasonable chance of making a difference?

4 Look for solutions

    (a) help groups to clarify and test understanding

    (b) facilitate stating of needs and desired outcomes

    (c) negotiate towards agreement.

181

5 Agree action

    (a) check that both parties have the same perception of the outcome

    (b) follow up action agreed.

CONFLICT HANDLING STYLES

Thomas and Kilmann (1974), suggest that certain styles of handling conflict are appropriate, depending on the circumstances and desired outcome. They differentiate between a confronting and non-confronting approach on one continuum, and a cooperative and non-cooperative approach on another continuum.

Collaborating

They suggest that a confronting, cooperative style is appropriate when it is important to find a solution where both sets of concerns are too important to be compromised, or where it is necessary to gain commitment by incorporating a number of views into a decision. This style takes time and effort, so may not be appropriate for issues which are trivial or unimportant. This is the style which fits most nearly with the problem-solving approach to negotiating.

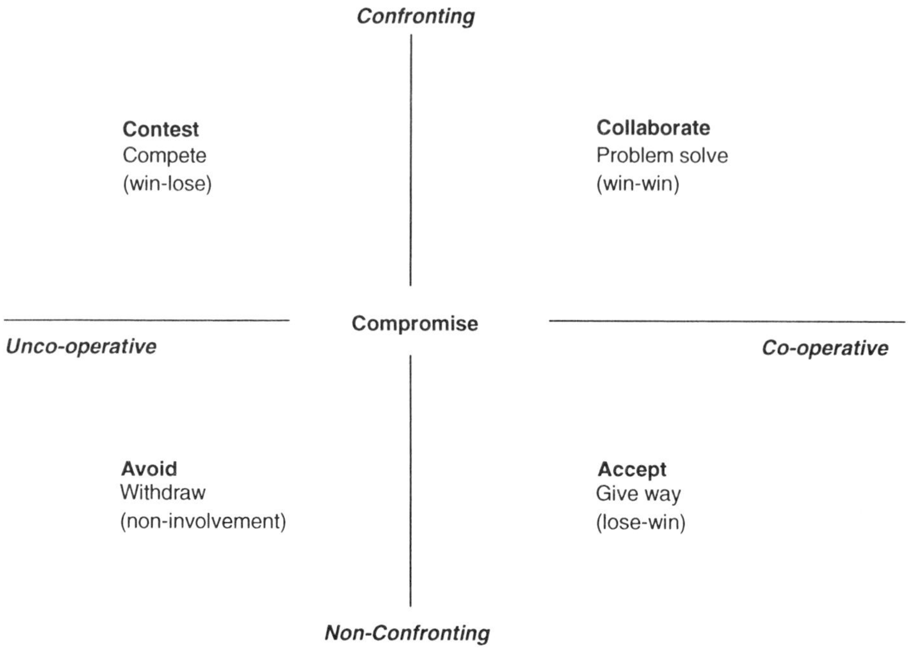

Confronting

Contest
Compete
(win-lose)

Collaborate
Problem solve
(win-win)

Compromise

Unco-operative

Co-operative

Avoid
Withdraw
(non-involvement)

Accept
Give way
(lose-win)

Non-Confronting

Fig. 14.1 Conflict handling styles

Contesting

A confronting, non-cooperative style may be appropriate when quick, decisive action is required, for example in emergencies, or on important issues where an unpopular course of action may need to be taken, (such as a directive from the powers that be) and there is no scope for taking other points of view into account.

Accepting

A non-confronting, cooperative style may be appropriate when you realise you are wrong, or the issue is much more important to the other person than yourself, or when you want to build up credit for the future. It means giving way to the needs, wants or demands of the other person involved and while it is wholly appropriate in some situations, it does tend to be a style which is over used by some and under used by others.

Avoiding

A non-confronting, non-cooperating style may be appropriate when an issue is trivial or when the benefit of confronting a conflict may outweigh the benefit of resolving it. Also, when the issue involved is one where you have low power and can see no chance of satisfying your concerns or making a change, such as national or some organisational issues, or personal idiosyncrasies.

Compromising

This style falls in the middle of all the others and has some elements of all of them. It is appropriate when goals are moderately important, but not so vital as to warrant more confronting methods, or when time pressures mean that you need to arrive at an expedient solution. It may mean that neither party is entirely happy with the outcome but is prepared to live with it. Although this style will certainly involve some negotiation and bargaining, it may be a quick exchange of concessions rather than leading to a solution which satisfies the needs of both parties.

All these styles are appropriate for certain situations, but a person is limiting their conflict handling ability if they are able to use only one or two styles comfortably. The ability to match the most appropriate conflict handling style to the situation means that conflict can be dealt with quickly and effectively.

183

Negotiating around conflict

BE AWARE OF THE DIFFICULTIES

If you are negotiating with the background of a previous or current conflict, the same stages, skills and strategies as you would normally use in a negotiation need to be applied, but certain things may be more difficult. It may be more difficult to take a problem-solving approach – the need to win may be uppermost in your mind. It may also be more difficult to take a rational look at what the other person involved might want – distortion creeps in more easily. The very approaches which will make it more likely that you will be able to negotiate an acceptable solution are those which are most difficult to do and also the most vital, if you have been involved in conflict. Being aware of the things which you may find most difficult may help you to do them despite your possibly antagonistic feelings towards the other people involved.

SIX POSITIVE STEPS

1 Take a problem-solving approach. Remember that if they can get something of what they want, you are more likely to get something of what you want.
2 Listen. Yes, listen to what they say. Don't sit there thinking of what

you want to say.

3 Question. Ask questions to find out more about their point of view or proposals. Ask questions to clarify issues and test your understanding.

4 Keep an open mind. Ask yourself 'What if' questions. Ask them 'What if' questions to help them see other options.

5 Remember that movement is the only way to make progress. It is your job to find ways for you to move towards them, and encourage and help them to move towards you.

6 Isolate the problem from the people involved. Concentrate on negotiating a solution and forget the personality of the person with whom you are negotiating

Negotiating with previous sparring partners

The last time that Howard and John negotiated, they did not have a happy experience. They were both determined that right was on their side and were not prepared to give an inch in the direction of the other person. The battle was bitter and bloody. When the negotiation broke down with acrimony on both sides, the affair was taken out of their hands by more senior management and settled to the satisfaction of neither party. They had both set out determined to win and both felt they had lost in the end.

In cases similar to, although perhaps not as extreme as this, where people have to negotiate with one another, already regarding each other as intransigent and wilful, it can be difficult to take a rational, problem-solving approach. Emotion colours your perspective on the problem, the importance of the issues, the people involved, their attitude, and so on.

Think grey, think slow, think quiet

The answer to this is to think grey, think slow, think quiet. When you think about the last time you dealt with the person or people concerned, you will unconsciously have a picture of what happened in your mind. Bring this picture into your conscious mind and see it on your TV screen. It will probably be in full colour, fast moving and loud. It may even be covered in a red haze! Whatever it looks like, think grey – turn the colours to pale greys and whites. Think slow – decelerate the action to slow motion. Think quiet – turn down the sound until you can hardly hear it. This technique will help you divorce yourself from the emotions implicit in your dealings with the people concerned and help you to focus on the Six Positive Steps which will result in an effective negotiation.

SUMMARY

Conflict tends to flavour many negotiations. Even when conflict is not immediately apparent, the potential for friction and confrontation, leading to conflict, exists. It is useful for negotiations to be aware of the reasons for and causes of conflict, and to be familiar with different approaches to handling conflict. Conflict can be constructive, but destructive conflict can cause far reaching damaging effects. Destructive conflict is often caused by lack of trust, or different perspectives to a situation or problem, and can be exacerbated by the difference in individual approaches to handling it. A small difference in opinion can escalate into conflict if it is not addressed. Use the following checklist to help you assess how best to address conflict.

Checklist

1 Find out the facts; the real issues, history, participants.
2 Identify the needs of both parties; find out what they really want and why they want it.
3 Assess the magnitude and level of the conflict. Does it need to be divided into manageable chunks; is it something you can do anything about?
4 Look for solutions; help groups to clarify issues and test understanding and facilitate the stating of needs and desired outcomes. Help them to negotiate towards agreement.
5 The most appropriate way to handle conflict might depend on the type of conflict and the circumstances. Check whether a collaborating, competing, accommodating, avoiding or compromising style is most appropriate.
6 When you are negotiating with the background of a previous or current conflict, take the Six Positive Steps to make it easier to achieve an acceptable solution.
   (a) take a problem-solving approach, remembering that if they can achieve something they want, you are more likely to get something you want
   (b) actively listen to them
   (c) ask questions to find out more information, clarify issues and test understanding
   (d) keep an open mind, asking yourself and them 'What if' questions to help you both look for other options
   (e) remember that movement is the only way to make progress
   (f) isolate the problem from the people involved. Concentrate on negotiating a solution and forget the personality of the person with whom you are negotiating.
7 When negotiating with previous sparring partners, think grey, slow and quiet to help to dissipate emotions and concentrate on the issue at hand.

15

Getting better all the time

It's getting better all the time . . .
. . . .
. . . and I'm doing the best that I can
I admit it's getting better
A little better all the time

The Beatles

So how do you ensure that your negotiations get a little better all the time? That each time you negotiate, you improve your skills and expertise? Negotiating, like many other skills gets easier the more you practise, but practice does not necessarily make perfect – though it may make it more effortless. If you are to improve every time you negotiate, you need to be able to learn from experience, from mistakes, from review and understanding of what went wrong and what went right.

In this chapter we look at:

- maximising your learning
- setting up your own practice exercises
- a summary of key elements in thinking on your feet in negotiations.

Maximising your learning

It is all very well to say learn from experience, but some of the things we learn from experience may be applied in negative and unhelpful ways. Early humans obviously learned that fire burns. If this had meant that they avoided fire at all costs because it was dangerous, the development of humankind might have taken a different path. Because early humans were able intelligently to modify the use of fire to be beneficial, their learning that fire burns was put to excellent use.

Kolb (1984), suggested that there is a cycle of learning. Learning entails having experiences, followed by thinking about and reviewing the experiences, followed by reflecting and drawing out some concepts and principles. Finally we test out the concepts in new situations, modifying them to suit our needs. This cycle can be simplified to the model in Fig 15.1. Honey and Mumford, using a similar model, suggested that different people learn best in different ways. Some individuals learn best by throwing themselves into having experiences, some prefer to look back at experiences and learn from them. Others prefer to learn from models and theories, and yet others learn from being able to apply theory to practice.

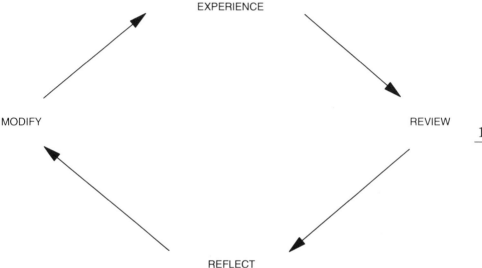

Fig. 15.1 The cycle of learning

Learning is most effective when all these stages are used. If you do have a tendency to prefer to learn in one way more than another, try incorporating all the stages of the cycle when you aim to improve your negotiating skills.

EXPERIENCE

Try it out. Put the theory into practice. If your manager isn't willing to let you loose on negotiations to decide the future of the company or the departmental budget yet, put some of the ideas into practice when you negotiate with your colleagues about where to go for lunch. The more often you practise a skill, the more comfortable it feels. When people ride a bicycle for the first time, most wobble and many fall off. It puts some people off for ever and they never ride a bicycle again. Others get back on, gradually the wobbling stops and they become proficient. Of course, some will become more proficient than others – while most will be capable amateurs, a few may go on to become long-distance or professional cyclists, the elite competing in international competitions such as the Olympics or the Tour de France – and of course there will be a few who always wobble slightly, but manage to get to their destination in one piece.

REVIEW

Think about it. When a number of people learn any skill, those who learn fastest think about how they did it last time and what the outcome was. What went well, what went wrong? Did the event progress in the way you expected, or were you taken aback or surprised by anything? How satisfactory for you was the outcome? At what points did your bicycle wobble and where did you fall off? Some useful questions to ask yourself at the review stage are:

1 What went well?
2 What (if anything) went badly wrong?
3 What could I have done differently?
4 What would I have liked to do better?
5 Did things go as planned?
6 How satisfactory was the outcome?
7 How different was the outcome from the one I would have liked?
8 What affected the outcome of the negotiation, positively or negatively?
9 Was it something that I did or something that they did?
10 How much did I shift from my original position?
11 How much did they appear to shift?
12 How much of my original outcome did I achieve?
13 Was it a win–win negotiation?

REFLECT

Continuing with the bicycle analogy, now begin to think about the reasons for the wobbling and the cause of the fall. Did you fall because the wobbling became so great that you couldn't control the bike any longer, or was it because you rode over a large stone? Was the wobbling caused by turning a corner, lack of balance or pure fear? Having looked at what went right and wrong in the reviewing stage, this is the time to think about the reasons for it. Why did it happen? How do the reasons relate to the knowledge you have about the skills and theories of negotiating? Some useful questions to ask yourself at the reflect stage are:

1 If it was win–win, what helped it to be so?
2 If it was not win–win, why not?
3 What did I do which helped towards a positive conclusion?
4 What helped them to move in my direction?
5 Which areas of preparation worked well and which did not?
6 What other active listening techniques could I have used?
7 What other questions could I have asked?
8 How could I have extended *my* thinking to help the other person extend theirs?
9 Could I have used any of the bargaining techniques such as *hmm – and*?
10 What might have happened if I had done any of these things?
11 Which area of background did I feel weak on?
12 Which other strategies, tactics or techniques could I have used?

MODIFY

Having reviewed your behaviour and reflected about what happened and the reasons for it, this is the stage to ask yourself what you could be doing differently in order to improve your performance. The crucial question to ask yourself at this stage, is, 'How will I do it differently next time?'

Some people get stuck at this stage, because 'the next time' with something like a negotiation may involve different people, different circumstances, different environment, and so on. So how, they ask, can you learn from one situation and apply that learning to a different situation?

1. You can plan how to do it differently next time. Some other points of preparation, a recognition of which strategies might be more appropriately applied, or an appreciation of how to deal with tactics which were used effectively against you, can help to make the next negotiation flow more smoothly.

2. The fact that you have reviewed and reflected on the previous negotiation will make your reactions sharper and more confident the next time you negotiate. Recognising that a particular question did not work in a specific circumstance can ensure that in the same circumstance you might ask a different question, or use the same question in a different way. Understanding that you may have been in too much of a hurry to reach agreement last time may mean that you are prepared to allow everyone to take a little longer this time.

3. If you asked yourself, 'What else could I have done?' you may be able to apply that 'What else' to the new situation. Reflecting on other skills you may have used means that they are at the top of your mind to be

189

used again. There are a number of things you can do to help use this model most effectively.

1 Be prepared to take some risks.
2 Ask for feedback from others.
3 Re-run the video.
4 Watch and analyse other negotiations.

Risk taking

Learning to do anything better often involves some risk. If no one took risks, nothing new or exciting would ever be accomplished. The risks you take need not necessarily be huge ones. They involve experimenting with techniques you may not have used before or being prepared to negotiate in areas where you may not have negotiated before. If you are worried, remember to think, 'What would be the worst that could happen?'

Feedback

Feedback from others can often be a valuable source of learning. Other people are often able to offer a different perspective or understanding of a situation, which can help in deciding which behaviour worked well and which might need to be modified in the future. It is not always possible to ask for feedback when you have been negotiating, but if you have been working with a team, other people have observed you, or you have been negotiating with someone where the relationship allows it, take the risk of asking for some feedback.

Feedback which is intended to be constructive is most helpful, but even where feedback is unasked for and negative, you can use it as an opportunity to improve your skills (and often disconcert the giver) by asking questions to direct the feedback to specific behaviour. Some of the questions you might use are:

> 'What specifically do you think could have been improved?'
> 'When you say 'that was a bit of a disaster', what specifically do you think was the problem?'
> 'Where precisely do you think that we took the wrong approach?'
> 'What makes you say that?'
> 'Could you explain what you mean a little more fully?'

Re-run the video

If you do not have the opportunity or courage to ask for feedback, try visualisation to help review the negotiation with more accuracy than just thinking about it. Imagine that you have a video of the whole negotiation. Re-run the scene through your head, seeing and hearing it on a television set in the corner of a room. This will give you a clear, sound basis for reviewing the episode. If you reach a place where things did not go as smoothly as you would have liked, slow the tape, watch and listen to exactly what happened. Now replace the behaviour you suspect caused the problem with the behaviour you wish you had used. Run the tape on to examine what the differences might have been if you had done that.

This is an excellent technique to help you move through the cycle of review, reflect and modify. It enables you to mentally put into practice the various modifications and think about the effects they might have had in the original situation. This in turn gives you a better idea of the effect they might have in the future.

Watch and analyse other negotiations

Watching other people can be useful if you use it as an opportunity to think about the techniques they use, the questions they ask, and to analyse the effect these questions and techniques have on the course of the negotiation and its outcome. It is essential to take an objective and discriminating view, focusing on the process of the negotiation rather than becoming involved in the content.

Set up your own practice exercises

If you would prefer to practise before tackling an 'important' negotiation, you can set up some exercises for yourself.

WORKING WITH OTHERS

Agree with some colleagues that you will set up some practice negotiations. If possible, choose something real, but unimportant to negotiate about. Some issues may be: who attends an unpopular meeting; who should get the next round of coffee; which charity should benefit from the money in the swear box; the date of the next meeting or report, etc.

The negotiation should be carried out as seriously as if the issue was vital. Think about your desired outcome and your ideal, realistic and fallback positions. Practise putting your case assertively and use the bargaining techniques which become appropriate. Be aware of tricks and threats and use questioning and listening skills to the best of your ability. Check that you have ensured implementation.

Then, with your colleagues, review and reflect on what was done well and what could have been improved. Give each other constructive feedback on the areas which were handled well and those which could

191

have been handled better. Help each other to think about how you could modify the behaviour, skills and techniques to improve next time round.

WORKING ON YOUR OWN

If you do not have the facility, time, or suitable colleagues to set up practice exercises, you can do a similar exercise by yourself. This means thinking ahead about the areas you are likely to have to negotiate on a day-to-day basis, and preparing yourself to treat them as the negotiations they are rather than a casual exchange. It is not as easy to review, reflect and modify on the negotiations you practise without colleagues to give you some feedback and extra insight, but it does mean that you take the opportunity to practise in 'safe' situations.

PRACTISING SOME SPECIFIC TECHNIQUES

Many of the techniques and skills discussed in this book can be used and practised outside negotiating. The specific techniques are mentioned in detail in the relevant chapters, but some which particularly lend themselves to rehearsal in day-to-day situations are:

- becoming aware of your power, external and internal
- behaving assertively
- building rapport, especially mirroring and matching
- summarising
- softening disagreement
- avoiding blaming, counter proposals, irritators, argument dilution
- testing understanding
- noticing body language
- painting a picture of how it could be
- *hmm – and*
- recognising threats
- active listening techniques
- many questioning techniques
- creative thinking and recognising the barriers which prevent you thinking creatively
- applying curiosity to new ideas
- taking a fly on the wall approach
- reframing
- using the learning cycle.

Key elements in thinking on your feet in negotiations

Approach

Taking a problem-solving approach means regarding a 'negotiation as a problem to be solved rather than a battle to be won. As you often need to continue living or working with people with whom you negotiate, this approach lays the groundwork for further contact and negotiation to be productive and positive. It need not be a one-sided approach to negotiating, as taking the lead often encourages others to adopt a similar strategy. Even if it is one-sided, looking for the solution to the problem rather than being hooked into a conflict is more likely to assist you towards achieving your desired outcome:

- separate the personality from the problem
- don't assume there is only one solution
- look for a solution, not a battle
- set it up to be constructive by summarising, questioning and showing your willingness to accept their point of view
- pull people away from win–lose and lose–lose approaches.

193

Preparation

Being properly prepared for a negotiation involves thinking about your own desired outcomes and needs, plus thinking about the possible demands, needs and outcomes of the other party. It is an essential part of the negotiation and may well take as long or even longer than the negotiation itself:

- know your desired outcome – what you want to achieve, why, is there only one way of achieving it?
- know your priorities and your limits
- establish your ideal, realistic and fallback positions. Estimate the bargaining arena
- know what concessions you can make and what you can barter
- know your strengths and weaknesses and the balance of power
- make educated guesses about their priorities, limits, strengths, weaknesses, outcomes. Estimate their ideal, realistic and fallback positions.

Power

The balance of power between two or more parties in a negotiation can affect the outcome of that negotiation. The environment, the situation and the perceptions of the individuals involved can affect and alter the balance of power. To make the most of your power in a negotiation, it helps to be aware of your own internal and external power and to have a realistic understanding of the power of your opponent in the particular situation.

Putting your case effectively

This involves putting across your message in a confident and assertive way, while being able to build and maintain rapport. Looking and sounding confident helps other people to believe in your competence. While aggressive or passive approaches may have short-term payoffs, an assertive approach will be more effective in achieving objectives. Building and maintaining rapport means that you are more likely to get what you want in a shorter time and to a higher standard:

- check how you look and how you sound
- check that you know what you want and that you can say 'no' effectively
- build rapport by mirroring posture and voice.

Skills and strategies

The skills and strategies used in successful negotiations help the process of bridging the gap between opposing parties and expediting a satisfactory conclusion. The level of skill and type of strategy used can make the difference between a long, tedious, bad-tempered negotiation and one which moves forward rapidly to an amicable conclusion:

- start positively, stating your objectives and asking for theirs
- ask for their opening position and state yours
- take time to think
- ask questions appropriately
- make an impact by drawing their attention and keeping the atmosphere positive
- avoid irritators, counter proposals, argument dilution and being drawn in to attack/defence spirals
- use behaviour labelling, testing understanding, saying what you feel and summarising
- assess offers against your realistic, ideal and fallback positions
- assess offers in terms of value, implementation and price.

Bargaining

Bargaining and trading separate negotiating from any other transaction between two or more parties. The process of bargaining facilitates movement of parties towards each other, and the essential skills of effective bargaining, giving and receiving signals, painting a picture of how it could be, trading and packaging are well worth polishing:

- brush up your awareness of signals sent by others, non-verbally and verbally
- be aware that you will be signalling unconsciously as well as consciously
- use phrases such as 'Suppose we . . .' and 'How would it be if' to create a vision of possible outcomes
- keep to the rules of trading to ensure that you get as well as give
- use the trader's phrase book *hmm – and, if . . . then*
- package demands and proposals to be able to give in one area while gaining in another.

195

Tactics, tricks and threats

These all form part of many negotiations, though not always a constructive part. Some tactics are useful, others need to be noticed and handled appropriately. Threats need to be used with caution and responded to with care and dexterity.

- adjournments are a useful tactic. Use them for assessing offers, gaining thinking time or cooling off time, checking facts and consulting colleagues
- only bluff if you are prepared to carry it through. Be prepared to take the risk of calling the bluffs of others
- don't be intimidated by the 'tough' stance. Stand up for your rights and stick to your problem-solving approach
- be prepared to challenge tactics which seem like a trick
- don't give in to threats unless you are left with no other alternative
- remember that if you make threats they have to be credible, that implementing them might impose a cost on you, that they have to be carried out to be believable and that they can escalate a dispute as often as they settle it.

Listening

Listening to what the other person has to say is such an obvious necessity in a negotiation. It is amazing how many negotiators do not use the potential of good listening. Instead they make assumptions, hear what they expect or want to, and talk too much. Good, active listening can make a difference to the quality of the information you receive, which in turn can make a difference to the outcome of the negotiation. It is relatively easy to improve your listening skill by practising active listening techniques in day-to-day conversations:

- use non-verbal behaviour and eye contact to show people that you are listening
- test your understanding and clarify meanings
- reflect back feelings and ask appropriate questions
- summarise.

Questioning

Questions are a versatile tool which are a vital part of the negotiating process, as they allow you to establish a wider framework for the negotiation, find your way out of stalemates, clarify details, stimulate thinking, gain commitment and float ideas. Improving your skill at using the basic questioning techniques which are familiar to most people and some of the less familiar questioning techniques, can add to the versatility of your negotiating:

- use open questions to encourage people to talk and closed ones to get short, 'yes' and 'no' answers
- use 'chunking up' questions such as 'What will having x do for you?' to get behind stated reasons for doing or wanting things
- use 'chunking down' questions such as 'How specifically?' or 'Exactly why?' to get at details and unpick generalisations
- challenge assumptions by asking 'What would happen if you did/ didn't?'
- don't accept statements at face value. Use probing questions to find out more detail
- stimulate thinking by asking 'What if?' or 'How would it be?'
- gain commitment by putting suggestions in the form of a question
- use questions as a way of defusing aggression and calming conflict.

Thinking

Thinking rapidly often seems to mean thinking in established ways and patterns, so that the rapid thought may not come up with any new or creative answers. Becoming more used to thinking creatively can extend the speed and ability of the brain to come up with new, different and sometimes better answers to a problem. Learning to think creatively means acknowledging the barriers to creative thought and consciously jumping over them.

- recognise the barriers to creative thinking such as patterns, fear of looking a fool, dominant ideas, polarising tendencies, tethering factors, boundaries and assumptions
- train yourself to use a number of questions to challenge assumptions and stimulate your thinking. For example 'What other ways?' 'Do we really need to?' 'Suppose that were not true?'
- Learn to reframe problems to see them in a different light
- take the worst consequence approach. What would be the worst that could happen? Would it matter if it did?

Dealing with the unexpected

Events don't always go the way that we anticipate. Unexpected circumstances, reactions, demands or opposition have the capacity to throw us off balance, or mean that we handle the situation less competently than we might otherwise have done. Learning to activate your rapid response mechanism when unexpected events arise can increase your ability to cope confidently.

197

- reduce fear of the unexpected by concentrating on your ability to handle the situation and giving yourself positive messages
- keep your cool in the way that suits you best. This may be thinking yourself into a calm state, counting to ten, or reframing the problem
- gain time by expressing your surprise, or repeating their statement back to them. Ask questions to clarify their outcome
- apply your natural curiosity, then look for evidence rather than applying the 'automatic no' to unexpected ideas or proposals
- accept unexpected cooperation gratefully if you are sure that there is no catch. Express your surprise and pleasure, but don't be afraid to ask questions and check the congruence between what they are saying and doing
- if you need to negotiate unexpectedly, gain extra thinking time if you can, and have an instant, limited outcome. Ask a lot of questions to establish as much of the background as possible and get a broader picture of the situation.

Stalemates

Stalemates seem to be an almost inevitable part of the negotiations we read about in the newspapers. The breakdown of talks, the recriminations and public blame seem to be an inescapable ingredient of most news bulletins. If a negotiation reaches the point where no further movement seems possible, it has arrived at stalemate. If nothing is done, all parties involved may dig themselves further and further into their entrenched positions, until deadlock is reached and charge and countercharge begin.

- use questions to gather new information which can help to unfasten all parties from the positions where they have become stuck
- apply a mental icepack to prevent you from feeling irritation or anger, while you turn your thoughts in a positive direction and begin to look for common ground
- summarise both positions and remind each other of the consequences of not reaching agreement
- address their concerns and find out why they might be stalling
- look for creative ways forward, chunking up or down, using questioning skills to move round the blockage, taking a fly on the wall approach, or mentally stepping into their shoes
- switch on your thinking, and use 'What if', reframing, worst consequence approach, metaphors or counter examples to switch on theirs
- if all else fails, fall back on your BATNA.

Conflict

Different approaches to conflict form the background of many a negotiation. Understanding the various reasons for conflict and the different ways you might react to it can help you assess how best to react in different situations. Individual approaches to handling conflict and the level which conflict has reached can affect the best way of handling it.

- address conflict by finding out the facts, identifying the needs of both parties, assessing the size and level, looking for solutions and agreeing action
- identify your own preferred conflict handling style and assess whether you are flexible enough to adapt your style to the situation or whether you tend to react in a similar way with all conflict
- take Six Positive steps to negotiating with a background of conflict: take a problem-solving approach, listen, question, keep an open mind, find ways to move and isolate the problem from the people involved.

Learning from experience

Use a learning loop to ensure that you learn each time you put any skill or technique into practice. Experience, review, reflect then modify your behaviour to maximise your learning. If you can set up opportunities to practise negotiating with colleagues or friends and give each other feedback and encouragement, do so. If this isn't possible, use any opportunity you can to practise specific skills and techniques, so that they feel comfortable and familiar when you use them in a negotiation.

Negotiating is fun. Go out and enjoy it.

Bibliography

■

Argyris, C, 1970, *Intervention Theory and Method: A Behavioural Science View*, Addison Wesley

De Bono, E, 1971, *Lateral Thinking for Management*, McGraw-Hill

Fisher, R and Ury, W, 1981, *Getting to Yes*, Arrow Books

French, J and Raven, B, 1959, 'The Bases of Social Power' in *Studies in Social Power*, (ed. Cartwright, D), Institute for Social Research of the University of Michigan

Handy, C, 1983, *Understanding Organisations*, Penguin Books

Honey, P and Mumford, A, 1982, *The Manual of Learning Styles*, Peter Honey

Honey, P and Mumford, A, 1983, *Using your learning styles*, Peter Honey

Kolb, D, 1984, *Experiential Learning*, Prentice Hall

Laborde, G. Z, 1983, *Influencing with Integrity*, Syntony Publishing

O'Connor, J and Seymour, J, 1990, *Introducing Neuro-linguistic Programming*, Mandala

Porter, Elias H, 1973, *Strength Deployment Inventory Manual of Administration and Interpretation*

Rawlinson, J. G, 1981, *Creative Thinking and Brainstorming*, Gower

Salaman, G, 1978, 'Management Development and Organisational Theory' *Journal of European Industrial Training*, vol 2, no 7

Taylor, D, 1986. 'Coping with Change' in *Planning and Managing Change*, (ed. Mayon-White, B), pp. 87–93, Harper and Row

Thomas, K. W and Kilmann, R. H, *Thomas-Kilmann Mode Instrument*, Xicom

Ury, W, 1991, *Getting Past No*, Business Books.

Index

■